Vratabandha Sanskaar, For the Confused Contemporary

By Prachi Datar Pendurkar

Published by: Prachi Datar Pendurkar

Ozone Evergreens, Harlur Road, Bangalore 560102

Pendurkar.prachi@gmail.com

www.snugbub.co.in

Printed in India, Edition 1

ISBN: 978-93-5777-066-8

"In Bharata, our *Rishis* have considered our Life as a journey to be celebrated. If Life is a journey, there are milestones that guide us through it and there are 16 major milestones given to us Bharatiyas by our Rishis and are commonly called Sanskaaras. Out of these, the 11th milestone in one's life is the *Upanayana*, also called the *Vratabandha Sanskara*. The word *"Upa"* means to bring close to or lead someone. *"Nayan"* is guiding someone and also an eye. When we combine these two words, what we get is- guiding someone and taking them close. Close to what? Many words in Sanskrit begin with *"Upa"*; by close examination, we can derive meaning from them. These words include *Upanishad, Upavaas, Upadesh, Upakarma, Upanyas* etc. All these words are associated with something that takes us closer to what is **beyond our sensorial and experiential selves**.

The idea of writing the book *"Vratabandha Sanskaar For the Confused Contemporary"* is one of the best things we have heard as *Gurukulam* Educators. Every child and every Family needs to be aware of what are the internal learning milestones of a child and nourish them with the right nutrition just like we nourish their physical bodies. There are enough and more details given in this book for anyone looking to understand all about this Sanskaar.

This is a wonderful compilation of elements of knowledge from an all-round perspective which is what every conscious contemporary Indian parent needs and seeks. In ancient times, the *Rishis* took up the role and responsibility of guiding young *Brahmacharis & Brahmacharinis*. They were also responsible for parenting them in their *Ashrams* and *Gurukulams*. Today as times change and the boundaries of roles and responsibilities are redefined, it is the need of the hour for parents to rise up and prepare themselves to become *Gurus* to their children and guide them through their *Brahmacharya*. A Guru is not someone who knows everything, but someone who never stops learning and is on the path of Self-Knowledge. As Prachi ji has beautifully put it out there, *Upanayana* is a wonderful opportunity for the entire family to learn and evolve to greater heights. Truly we hope every family makes the best use of this compilation."

Deepti Hasabi & Lakshman Easwaran

Curriculum Developers & Mentors at Sanatana Life Academy

"The message this book brings out is extremely important and unique. The author is talking about a new, rather evolved way of giving the Sanskaar to the child. She is helping families to merge traditions with contemporary actions to shape good students and human beings. It's quite interesting as the child will be equally involved in following the *Vratas* and the thread ceremony won't be just a milestone that people do for the sake of doing."

Mugdha Hasabnis

State award winner Playback singer, Music Composer, and Lyricist

"I want to congratulate Prachi that she felt the urge to write on such a subject which is totally forgotten these days. Most people perform this ritual as an event to celebrate without knowing the importance of this ritual. In the first part, she has nicely written about the 'Varnashram system' which was purely based on your skills and not on caste. As mentioned in the book, circumstantially it became a ritual only for Brahman boys. I would like to give one example here. Vishwamitra was born as a Kshatriya. He was a king. But inspired by Bramharshi Vashishtha he did *tapas* to get higher knowledge and became a great *Rishi*. Vratabandha Sanskaar was performed in his case as well.

As Prachi rightly this *Sanskaar* is a type of oath taken by a student that he will stay away from all types of temptations and focus on his studies. Nowadays students have many temptations and Sanskaar can be very helpful for all.

In the second part, she speaks about the relevance of this ritual in these modern times. I was very much impressed by the perspectives she has brought in. This is a must-read for all young parents."

Smt. Rewati Kulkarni

Astrologer, Educator, Writer

"व्रतबंध या संस्काराबद्दलची सौ. प्राची पेंडुरकर यांची ही पुस्तिका अतिशय अभ्यासपूर्ण झालेली आहे.कुठलेही काम

करण्यापूर्वी चकित्सिक आणिजिज्ञासू वृत्तीने त्याचा अर्थ समजावून घेऊन मग करणे या दृष्टीने व्रतबंध या विषयावरचे हे लेखन हा एक सतुत्य उपक्रम आहे.

मानव हा संस्काराने श्रेष्ठ होत असतो. योग्यवेळी योग्य त्या वयात योग्य ते संस्कार झाले की माणसाच्या जीवनाला योग्य तो आकार येतो. ह्या अनुषंगाने मनुष्यावर करण्यात येणाऱ्या सोळा संस्कारांपैकी उपनयन किंवा व्रतबंध हा संस्कार अत्यंत महत्त्वाचा आहे. नेमकेपणाने अभ्यास करून संशोधक वृत्तीने लहिलिले हे पुस्तक या संस्काराबद्दल नव्या पढीला जागरूक करण्याचे काम करेल असा मला विश्वास वाटतो."

Smt. Vidya Dugal

Purohit, Recipient of 'Nation Builder Award', by Rotary Club, Nasik.

"This book delves into a topic which seems to have been distorted extensively through the ages. Though as a practice it is still performed today, in most families it seems to be carried through without much actual research, more as a formality and as a matter of just going with tradition.

While there is only that much that English as a language can do justice to in topics such as these which can only truly be understood through original Sanskrit vocabulary and true meaning, a brilliant attempt has been made to demystify this topic and full credit to Prachi Pendurkar for her attempt at thoroughly researching and publishing this as a book for reference. The importance of initiation of a child into true 'Vidya' so to speak, and as it was earlier practiced, into *Gurukulam* as an institution of study, has been beautifully and clearly brought out here. In the last thousand years, amidst the scores of attempts to denounce and destroy Sanatana dharma, the *Gurukulam* as an institution has also suffered immensely. However, whenever one makes a sincere attempt to reach out to divinity, the tenets of Sanatana dharma automatically present themselves as the only true teachings which are available to the one who is truly ready to receive them. This book is also a wonderful manifestation of Sanatana dharma, which is available to those who are truly ready to receive the teachings."

Dr. Shruti Jayasurya & Srinivas Abhinav Raj

Pediatric Dentist & Software Engineer

***

PREFACE

They said, "Kids will turn 8 next year, so when are you planning your boy's thread ceremony?"

"No way! How is it relevant today? Just because we are born in a Hindu family? I am an agnostic. I don't want to put my kids through this drama. Wearing awkward clothes in front of all, sitting in front of the fire, begging for food, all this for what? To please society? People feast, leave and the family earns social acceptance, that's all?" I immediately questioned.

He (husband) said, "I don't think it is right to comment on something we have incomplete information about. Anyways why are you such a rebel? I would not indulge in a fight with the family. For everyone's sanity, we can just get done with the ritual. But since you clearly don't seem to agree, take some time and do your research. Post that let's discuss if we want to go ahead with the ceremony or not"

"Valid and challenge accepted", I said. And thus began my journey into inquiry.

How many of you are sailing in the same boat? I am sure many, and many more will in the future. As I started the research using various resources, I earned a wealth of knowledge. About the educational systems, ways of life, religions, and more.

I started compiling my findings. I thought, not everyone will have the same time, opportunity, and resources to invest in similar research. Keeping this in mind, I decided to make my work accessible to all. That's how this book was born. The book is a mix of facts, reflections, and ideas. The subjective content may or may not sync with you 100%. With time and changes in circumstances, that is bound to happen. All I wish through this book is to provide a perspective to parents, caregivers, and prospective parents. The book aims to decode the Why, What, How, When and more of the Vratabandha Sanskaar. The book ideates on how we can make the Sanskaar meaningful for new-age families.

Another revelation during the process- Education in the current system is so superficial! 'Born in a pious family, having secured so-called 'crème de la crème' qualifications, why I am so blank when it comes to knowing about our ways of life?' Isn't it shameful, I thought, that I cannot answer this basic question "What is Hinduism?", "What are the principles of Sanatana Dharma, and do you follow them?". We are conditioned to look at western ways as superior to ours and are conditioned to look at the west as aspirational1. The root cause is not arrogance or malafide intentions – WE (Our Generation) ARE IGNORANT! We know so little about our own history and facts.

This book is a humble attempt to share my learnings, thoughts, and knowledge for the benefit of all. I do not claim to be an authority on this topic. The book does not aim to judge anyone for the choices they make. It is not a directive that a particular religion is superior to others, or that old ways were the best. It is important to make informed choices, adapt with time, and filter out what is not relevant.

You can share your feedback or your thoughts at Pendurkar.prachi@gmail.com or @tejas_prachi on Instagram.

***

---

[1] Palki Sharma, Macaulay Education System, Colonialisation & Inferiority complex in India Explained, https://youtu.be/SEseHkMwPSM

INTRODUCTION

The Vratabandha Sanskaar ("VBS") is one of the most prominent of the 16 Sanskaars. It carried huge significance and was considered the child's second birth. But today, when this topic comes up in a social setting or family discussions, we generally come across three categories of responses:

- We must do it since it is a part of our tradition and an important religious ritual;

- This ritual is obsolete, we should not do it; or

- This ritual is applicable only to Brahmin boys; hence it is not applicable in other cases.

These three categories of people have their own set of questions and confusions. The book aims to cater to them all! The book addresses fundamental questions of VBS like:

- What is the significance of VBS?

- Who is it applicable to?

- When is it to be done? etc.

It also questions some of the elements of VBS which are obsolete and need changes to suit today's needs!

What picture comes to your mind when you think of VBS? If you have attended any, it is mainly a ritual, where the boy has to go through certain steps, like a public bath, shaving his head, fire worship etc. Traditional food, family photos, dressed-up crowd, exchange of gifts et all are the ceremonial aspects attached to VBS.

The boy is; sometimes happy (because of all the attention), many times feels awkward (due to the various processes involved), and at times excited (many boys are bribed with fancy gifts for cooperating). But at the bottom of it all, the boy is clueless about what is happening! VBS has in most cases remained as a formality, a celebration for many, and a status symbol for some, without understanding the underlying meanings2.

Having understood this, and looking at the current education system, does VBS carry the same relevance as before? Maybe not. But it has a lot of other aspects attached to it, which can still be held relevant and useful. VBS when done thoughtfully can be a transformative experience for the family. Through the book, I hope to uncover the underlying meaning of VBS and make it relatable to the contemporary.

An act for our children which is meaningful, logical, and beneficial is happily welcomed by society. After

---

[2] Sri Ramanasramam- Upanayanam, https://ramana-talk-mailer.appspot.com/read?post_name=Letter&index=124

all, we want the best for our children. I assure you that you will find some pearls of information, direction, and pointers in the coming chapters. Let's hope our parenting styles, education systems, and social fabric enables holistic development for children in the future. It will, hopefully, leave them less confused than us! Let the Foundation for the next generation be 'सत्यम शविम सुंदरम'.

***

HOW TO NAVIGATE AND USE THIS BOOK

- The book is mainly divided into two parts:

  Part 1: The Basics: This part mainly provides information, and reasoning behind some practices, and throws light on what is currently being done.

  Part 2: The Brain Teasers: This part talks about how to adapt and evolve VBS based on changing needs and situations. How to make VBS relevant and fruitful for our next-gen and a transformative experience for the family.

- The phonetic spellings of Sanskrit and Hindi words have been put into *Italics font* wherever applicable.

- Both sections have content in Question-Answer format, so you can easily jump onto the relevant question as need be.

- For ease of reference, a child has been addressed as him/his/he, however, this is not to restrict the scope of the book to the male gender only and needs to be interpreted in a gender-neutral way.

- Some of the procedures or finer details are bound to vary as compared to what you have seen or known based on your location/ Purohit/ culture etc. My request here would be to focus on the underlying message rather than debating over procedural aspects of it. Look at the bigger picture ▯

- Wherever possible appropriate **references** have been mentioned. The references do not just serve the purpose of substantiating the statements, but are a **resource in itself**, should anyone want to read further on the topic.

***

PART 1: THE BASICS

WHAT IS VBS, AND WHAT WAS ITS SIGNIFICANCE?

Let us travel back in time. Centuries behind us, when India's literacy rate was at its peak, India was a learning hub and attracted students from across the globe[3]! Yes, back then, the *Gurukul* Education system ("GES") was robust. Education was given the topmost priority, irrespective of the gender, caste, or religion one followed[4]. *Gurukulams* can be explained as learning centers/ boarding schools, equipped with able teachers (*Gurus)* who dedicated their entire lives for this purpose. Yes, education was a serious affair, a non-negotiable rather.

Children on reaching a particular age and when seen ready would leave their homes and go to the *Gurukulams* where they would spend

---

[3] Sahana Singh (2017), The Educational Heritage of Ancient India How An Ecosystem of Learning Was Laid to Waste, pg 2.

[4] Immortal Bharat, Part 1 - Education in Ancient India, https://youtu.be/M79C3dSB90A.

minimum 10 to 15 years. Education, unlike today, was a full-time activity. The learning centers were located away from the hustle and bustle of civilizations, in calm places, and surrounded by nature. This distance was probably purposeful, to reduce the distractions for students and provide the right environment to focus on their skills. Education was in itself a *Tapas,* a rigorous process that yielded a huge amount of respect in society upon completion.

The below popular Sanskrit *Subhashitam* narrates the importance of education. It states that a person who is not educated, not only loses wealth but also loses healthy social relationships and in turn happiness.

अलससूय कुतो वदि्या, अवदि्यसूय कुतो धनम्,

अधनसूय कुतो मति्रम्, अमति्रसूय कुतो सुख: ।

It was believed that education is life learning and was holistic in nature. It demanded a certain level of discipline to help the children stay focused and gain expertise in different walks of life. Education focused on the wisdom from *Vedas,* and also covered multitude of subjects like mathematics, astronomy, physics, chemistry, spirituality, and more based on child's interests and needs[5]. A child would typically spend about 10 to 15 years in this learning journey.

Imagine a span of 10-15 years, where there is no concept of weekdays and weekends, but learning happens at each step. Through play, structured lessons, cooking, cleaning, and all the daily chores. Imagine giving up the luxuries of being with your families and instead growing up with learned *Gurus,* learning with peers, and doing projects with kids of varied ages[6]. It sounds exciting, but at the same time overwhelming,

---

[5] Aditya Singh, Subjects Taught in Gurukul Education System, https://vediconcepts.com/subjects-taught-in-a-gurukul/

[6] Shri Rajiv Dixit, Macaulay Destroyed Ancient Indian (Guru-Shishya) Education System, https://www.youtube.com/watch?v=q9N68QDyEbl&t=1143s

isn't it? And hence it did require a certain level of mental and physical preparation before the child set out to the *Gurukulams*.

Let us understand how this progression of a child-to-student worked. An ideal human life span of 100 years was typically divided into five stages: *ShishuAwastha, BrahmacharyaAshram GrihasthAshram, Vanaprastha Ashram,* and *SanyaasAshram* as follows:

Stage of Life	Rough Age Range	Main Features of the stage
0.Shishu Awastha	0-7	Making sense of the world around, learning to take care of basic needs like eating, cleaning oneself, taking care of one's elimination cycles, movement, and speech.

1.Brahmacharya Ashram	*8-25*	Holistic Education, Health, Spirituality.
2.Grihastha Ashram	*26-50*	Earning livelihood through rightful ways, raising a responsible next generation, caring for family and society.
3.Vanaprastha Ashram	*51-75*	Using skills and savings for the betterment of society.
4.Sanyaas Ashram	*76-100*	Spiritual advancement and leading a minimalist life.

During the early years, the child mainly spent time in the care and comforts of the family. The concept of babysitting, preschools, daycares, etc. was non-existent then! The early years were spent with the family, learning to communicate, understand social norms, understand relationships, and slowly moving towards the need to be literate. Primary caregivers played an important role in strengthening the wings of the child, preparing the child for the upcoming challenges in life.

The child while growing up, was observing, how the *Annas* and *Akkas* after a certain age move to *Gurukulams* and was observing how people progress from one stage of life to another. This observation prepared the child mentally to align with the life progressions effortlessly. In *ShishuAwastha,* the child mastered life skills of eating by oneself, taking care of basic hygiene, personal care, and elimination. The child then naturally expressed a desire to learn and do new things. This indicated the child's **physical and mental readiness** to move to the next level- *BrahmacharyaAshram*!

Once the child was ready to move to the *BrahmacharyaAshram,* this transition from *ShishuAwastha* to *BrahmacharyaAshram* was marked by VBS! Just like marriage is a transitional ritual between celibacy and married life, VBS was the **transitional ritual** between early childhood and celibacy.

VBS is also known by different names like thread ceremony, *Janeu, Vidyavrat, Upanayanam, Munja, Yadnyopavit, Vratabandha, Poonal etc.* The literal meaning of *Upanayan*am is 'taking near', where the *Guru* is taking the child near him as a disciple. And *Vratabandha* means bound by vows. A boy who is eligible for VBS is referred to as *Batu* and the girl is referred to as *Brahmavadini*.

VBS thus serves **three** objectives:

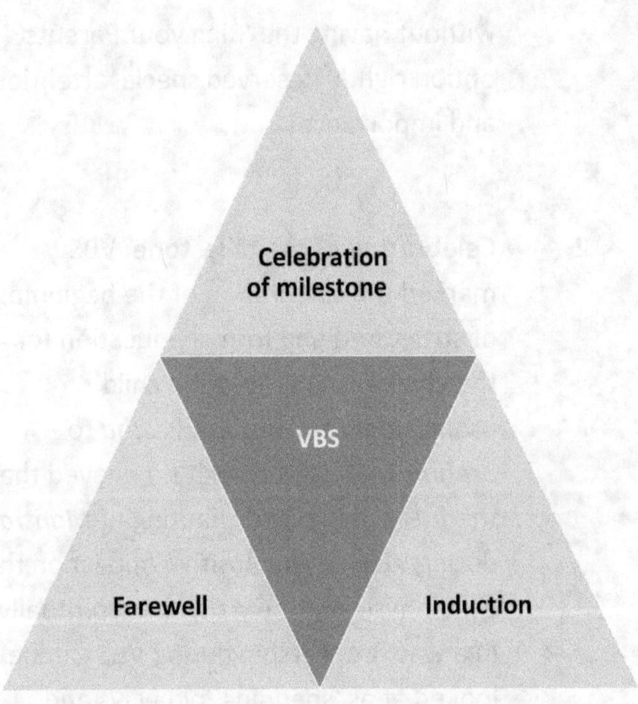

1. **A Farewell**: The child had to leave his house and move to the *Gurukulam* after VBS like a baby bird taking his first flight when the wings are strong enough. Thus, VBS acted as a farewell to the child. There are several rituals in VBS where the child is pampered by the mother and family. Farewell of a child at a young age, to a distant place, with unfamiliar people,

without having the 'Ring your Parents' option rightly deserved special attention and importance!

2. **Celebration of the milestone:** VBS marked the celebration of the beginning of structured and formal education for the child. It celebrated the child's promotion from *ShishuAwastha* to *BrahmacharyaAshram*. It is believed that the fire worship and chanting of *Mantras* during VBS leave a positive impact on the child physically, mentally, and spiritually. In a way fire worship during VBS can be looked at as 'shedding' old ways and embracing the new ones.

3. **Inducting the child into the new phase of life:** Schools organize an 'Open House' before the actual school begins, to help parents and students understand the basic rules and regulations of the place. When a person joins a new company, the person undergoes an induction process, to help him familiarize himself with the

ways of the workplace. Similarly, VBS acts like an **'Induction'** before the child steps into *BrahmacharyaAshram*. Various steps in VBS aim towards this objective, including the *Vratas* which the child agrees to follow.

Thus VBS, was looked at as the second birth of the child. The *Sanatana Dharma* lists 16 *Sanskaars* that hold an important place in one's life. Though some of them have become obsolete, VBS continues to be important even now. The 16 *Sanskaars* (important milestones of life) as per the *Sanatana Dharma* are[7]:

Sr. No.	Name of the *Sanskaar*	Short Description
1.	*Garbhadhaan*	Ritual on conception

---

[7] Rajbali Pandey (2018), Hindu Samskaras; Socio-Religious Study of the Hindu Sacraments, pg 23

2.	*Punsavan*	Prayers for the healthy growth of the fetus
3.	*Seemantonayan*	Similar to a baby shower
4.	*Jatkarma*	Ritual at birth
5.	*Naamkaran*	Naming ceremony
6.	*Nishkramana*	The first movement of the infant outside the house
7.	*Annaprashan*	A child having solid food for the first time in life
8.	*Chaul*	Shaving head
9.	*Akshar Abhyasa*	Introduction to writing and literacy
10.	*Karnavedh*	Ear piercing
11.	*Vratabandha*	The transition from Level 0 to Level 1 of life

12.	*Vedarambha*	Starting the study of *Vedas*
13.	*Keshanti*	Shaving hair and beard
14.	*Samavartana*	Graduation
15.	*Vivaha*	Marriage
16.	*Shraddha*	The last rites

Another interesting fact is that VBS, in many cases, was not just a one-time activity[8]. It was repeated if the circumstances changed. For example, if the child progressed to another *Guru*, or when the child progressed to a different stream of education.

But what happens today? Today, the ritual is done as a formality or for social acceptance or to

---

[8] Rajbali Pandey (2018), Hindu Samskaras; Socio-Religious Study of the Hindu Sacraments, pg 116

carry forward the traditions, or as a reason to get together and celebrate.

In most cases, the child is clueless as to what is happening and why. Unlike those times, we have a completely different education system, a completely different lifestyle, and a completely different social structure. Life progressions are not prominently visible like then. In these circumstances when VBS is performed as a copy-paste, it is not going to be meaningful either.

***

IS VBS APPLICABLE ONLY TO CERTAIN CASTE/ GENDER?

One-word answer: **No!**

But to understand that, we need to first understand how the society was structured. It was way different than what we see today! It was a simple system of *Varnas*. *Sanatana Dharma* describes four *Varnas* (occupations/ sects): *Brahmin*, *Kshatriya*, *Vaishya*, and *Shoodra*. The roles of each *Varna* are described below:

Varna	**Primary Nature of work based on Qualities and Interest**
Brahmin	Education, Priestly duties
Kshatriya	Administration, safety, and security
Vaishya	Trade and commerce
Shoodra	Service sector

A person was born in a *Varna,* true, but the person had the right to choose the *Varna* based on one's qualities and inclination[9]. Each *Varna* had its own roles and responsibilities and a place in the system. Without all four *Varnas* being in harmony, a system could not function well.

If you closely look at the four *Varnas*, you will notice that the *Brahmin Varna* had the responsibility of education, religious and spiritual activities. Thus, having an in-depth **knowledge of Vedas** and other scriptures was the **topmost occupational need**. In many cases, the child's father took the role of a *Guru,* and learning started 'In-House' before moving to the *Gurukulam*. VBS being the passport to Vedic studies, was thus performed earlier in these cases.

For other *Varnas,* literacy and Vedic knowledge were important, no doubt, but what took priority was skill building. For example, the son of the potter would spend more time learning about pottery, trying to work with mud and clay, and other tools, as he would also be exposed to them

---

[9] Pradnya Jere & Y. S. Lele (2003), *Dharmavidhinchya Antarangat,* Sanskrit Sanskriti Sanshodhika, pg 58.

from early childhood. Kids of other *Varnas*, typically joined *Gurukulam* at a later stage. They would spend those years with the family, specializing in their respective areas like art, administration, trade, agriculture etc. Literacy and study of Vedas thus came later in the hierarchy. Hence VBS for children belonging/ choosing other *Varnas* happened a little later in life (not beyond 24 years, however[10]).

This also throws light on how important skill-building was at that time. A lot of importance was given to doing hands-on work, learning through play, learning through observation, etc., which is now looked at as 'modern ways of learning'. That was the time when skill-building and literacy went hand in hand. For the *Brahman Varna*, however, both being synonymous, formal education started sooner than other *Varnas* and thus VBS too.

---

[10] *Rashtra Sevika Samiti (2011), Upanayan Sanskaar, Shodh va Bodh,* pg 34.

Education in those times was for all. There was no gender or *Varna-driven* bias[11]. Education was truly free of discrimination. Girls, boys, and kids from all backgrounds had the right to education and studied together. **VBS was performed for both boys and girls**[12][13]. There is enough evidence of girls being equally competent and well-read in those times. During the times of invasions, women's education and freedom got a massive setback. The rich culture of complementary gender balance moved towards patriarchy. *Jati* system took over the *Varna* system which led to unreasonable and unfair rules by the self-proclaimed superiors. Our beautiful GES started crumbling!

Talking about today, we no more have a *Varna* system. People choose occupations based on their will, opportunities, and interests. We have freedom to **choose,** which is great! We see so

---

[11] Sahana Singh (2022), Revisiting the Educational Heritage of India, Vitasta Publishing Pvt. Ltd. Pg 142

[12] V. L. Manjul, Starting Vedic Studies, https://www.hinduismtoday.com/magazine/october-november-december-2002/2002-10-starting-vedic-studies/.

[13] Sahana Singh (2022), Revisiting the Educational Heritage of India, Vitasta Publishing Pvt. Ltd. Pg 72

many *Brahmins* (born in a *Brahmin* family) who do not work in educational or religious sectors. Similarly, many others take up educational, and religious activities for their livelihood. There is no logical reason why anyone should be denied the right to VBS based on which caste/ creed one belongs to! It was never the case in the times of GES, there is **no merit** in enforcing such baseless **restrictions** today either! All it creates is division and conflicts- for no reason!

Education today is for all. After independence, we see various Government initiatives to promote education. Special focus is given to the education of the **female gender**. Walls painted with slogans like 'बेटी बचाओ, बेटी पढ़ाओ', are plentiful! When education is for all, how can VBS be restricted to only a particular gender? When one understands the roots of VBS, this **discrimination seems utterly baseless.**

If we go back to the basic objectives that VBS serves:

1. Farewell
2. Celebration of Milestone
3. Induction to the next level

The whole *Sanskaar* focuses on the **child and education!** Over the years, it got painted in the color of religion, caste, and gender, and VBS lost its true meaning. VBS in its true sense is beyond the innumerable divisions made by us humans.

If you see meaning in VBS, do it for your child. Do it without fear of being judged. Do it without the fear of man-made boundaries. If you align with the above progression of life, if you feel education is important, if you feel focused education needs a level of dedication and preparation, VBS is relevant for you. It is time we revive it! It is time we look at VBS as a beautiful tool to shape a better tomorrow!

"For you and for me and the entire human race"

***

WHAT MADE VBS A 'BRAHMIN-BOY' ONLY RITUAL?

The answer lies in our history.

When it comes to survival, everything else takes a back seat. Centuries of **invasions**, physical destructions, exploitations, inhuman activities, divide and rule policies, wiped out our *Gurukulams* and crumbled our foundation- our GES. It then led to a domino effect. Our robust systems got severe blows for centuries!

In a situation where you are under someone else's control, when life is at stake, what becomes a priority is personal safety. A family who could manage to stay safe could then move to the next 'to-do' of earning a livelihood. Education clearly would be the least important aspect in such a situation. **Survival** first then comes thriving!

This was also the time when women's education took a massive setback. With an intention of safeguarding women, who were easy targets for oppression and torture, women became homebound. Over the safety of themselves, and their young ones, and with the education system collapsing, the importance of women's education faded.

Let us understand what happened during the British era. As we know the *Gurukulams* were open for all genders and *Varnas*. There was no fee structure and the students would offer a *Gurudakshina* to the *Guru* on graduation based on their will and feasibility. There was absolutely no discrimination. We had a literacy rate of a whooping 97-100%[14]! In 1835, T. B. Macaulay surveyed GES and realized "As a field should be fully plowed before a crop is planted, GES must be plowed and an English education system must be introduced." This would offer the British an army of *Hindustani* bodies with English minds on an ongoing basis! Then came The **English Education Act** which turned out to be the final nail in the coffin. *Gurukulams* became illegal in India! With physical demolitions, harassment of

---

[14] Shri Rajiv Dixit, Macaulay Destroyed Ancient Indian (Guru-Shishya) Education System, https://www.youtube.com/watch?v=q9N68QDyEbI&t=1143s.

Gurus, heavy taxes, and all the adverse conditions created, it was impossible for GES to function[15]. It made it nearly impossible to continue education in native languages. Rest is history.

In these times, people whose livelihood was skill driven than literacy driven, started focusing on skill-building and earning. Thus, for the *Varnas,* other than the *Brahmin Varna*, literacy, and education were nowhere on the priority list. For the other *Varnas,* learning Vedas thus became redundant and irrelevant. All that mattered was to upskill in the area of work, deliver and earn. Formal education stopped.

The essence of *Brahmin Varna* was all about engaging in religious, and educational activities. Knowledge of *Vedas,* and scriptures, and being literate was **the only skill** and tool they had for their livelihood. Doing anything else was alien. Also, the other *Varnas* continued to need support from *Brahmin Varna* for their religious

---

[15] Immortal Bharat, https://www.immortalbharat.in/2020/07/how-british-destroyed-indian-education.html

activities. Hence the age-old ways of *Vedic* education slowly turned into a *Brahmin-only* activity, in a family-centric setting or small groups. And VBS thus continued for the *Brahmin* boys before commencing Vedic education. This is how slowly VBS turned into a ***Brahmin* boy-only ritual**. But as you see this was purely **circumstantial**.

The British, with the intention of creating local laborers who understood their language, and who worked loyally for them, introduced English medium schools in India. India started filling up with English medium schools that offered incentives, job security, and a better standard of living to people enrolling here. People were compelled (initially) or encouraged to send their children to these schools. This strategy worked wonderfully for the British! Soon these schools became mainstream. With access to education, food security, and better living conditions, people found a new ray of hope in the English education system.

Respect for the learned, who knows the *Vedas* and other scriptures, is deeply rooted in our culture. The *Brahmins* were treated with tremendous respect and love for their knowledge of Vedas. They were looked at as the 'superior' ones on this basis. The British took advantage of this and started creating a divide in society, which of course worked as we all know! British also used the 'Aryan – Dravidian invasion theory' (a myth which is established by mere force of repetition) to cut down Indians' pride in their past and culture[16]. A lot of religious conversions from Hindus to Christians happened during this time. Thus, it turned out to be a **'Divide – Convert - Rule'** mission for the British.

Sections of society claiming superiority became rampant. *Brahmins* who received respect for being the learned class started to claim superiority over others. Men claimed superiority over women for being educated. The ones learning English claimed superiority over the others, and so on.

This also led to a diffusal of the *Varna* system and *Jati* system took over. Children in schools were grouped together based on age and not

---

[16] Michel Danimo (Third Edition 2011), The Invasion That Never Was, Vivekananda Kendra Prakashan Trust, pg 20.

ability or interest. Individual, skill-based learning diminished, and a cookie-cutter approach to education developed. Learning *Vedas* and scriptures became 'Out of syllabus', and has almost turned alien today!

Years after years, generations after generations, these 'diversions' from the original taken in 'survival mode' started getting normalized! A society that once was the richest in terms of educational systems, tuned into a society where gaining basic literacy became a luxury and English degrees became a matter of pride!

Today we are completely whitewashed and believe in statements like "The English brought education to India"! Whereas the truth is something else! Forget the revival of GES, even if the true history is brought out in the history lessons for our children, it would be a big achievement and a great gift we can give generations to come. After all our national motto is!

सत्यमेव जायते ।

***

WHO CAN PERFORM VBS FOR THE CHILD?

During GES, it was the *Guru* who performed VBS for the child. But today it is the father who performs this *Sanskaar* for the child with the help of a *Purohit*.

Let us understand the reasoning, and the thought process behind this.

The mother in normal circumstances is the primary caregiver for the child in the initial years. With more awareness about co-parenting, fathers are also involved in the upbringing of the child from the early days. Even then, mothers assume a bigger chunk of responsibilities in the early years of development. As the child gets more self-reliant, the need for physical caregiving diminishes. The child slowly is able to take care of his basic needs like food as well as elimination cycles. This is when the role of the father slowly starts assuming more importance in the form of '*Guru* on call'. Hence in VBS, the child's father assumes a significant role as he steps into the shoes of a *Guru*.

Another perspective, on why the child's father would perform VBS was that: mothers, at the thought of the child leaving the house for a decade or more, would be in a **different and difficult mental state**. This state of the mother's wandering mind would make it more difficult for the child to stay calm through VBS. Hence in many places, the mother is advised not to be present at the scene during VBS. This practice is followed even now! However, in today's times, this is **no more relevant**. The majority of children are growing up in the care of their parents.

Keeping aside gender bias is also important considering **diverse family structures** with different compositions. For example, families with two mothers, two fathers, single mothers, adopted children, etc. to name a few. Thus, the decision as to who will perform VBS for the child should be a decision made by the family and *Purohit*, **without gender bias**.

Insisting on having only the father perform VBS or treating it as an eligibility criterion for VBS is not a practical approach. **Any primary caregiver** of the child is in the right position to perform VBS for the child along with the *Purohit*.

***

WHO IS A *PUROHIT*?

A *Purohit* is a **bridge** between the scriptures and the common man. Sadly, with the kind of modern education, and other socio-political dynamics, the role of *Purohit* is looked at from a very narrow lens. It is limited to someone who chants *mantras*, professionally helps accomplish the ritual and is paid in return. In the true sense, he is the **facilitator** who can be the right guide, help us understand the real deeper meanings of the rituals, and also help with the ceremonial aspects of the *Sanskaar*.

The need of the day is to have *Purohits*, who not just do the 'job' but are open and capable to tweak and modify the rituals to suit contemporary situations and needs. Hence the role of a *Purohit* is very important.

For VBS too, the *Purohit* acts as an instrument to perform the rituals and helps the child understand the underlying meaning.

While this occupation is still male dominated, there are many progressive organizations that teach aspiring people to take *Paurohitya,* without a specific qualification or bias. Even a family member can choose to get trained in this area and take up the role of a *Purohit*. However, some characteristics that can define a righteous *Purohit* are[17]:

- Has undergone VBS for oneself. This covers the 'experience' element.
- Dedication and mastery in the subject, Vedic wisdom, understanding of Sanskrit language, and communication skills.
- To be non-discriminative. A *Purohit* should not deny services to others based on caste, creed, color, or any other differences.
- To follow a certain level of discipline and values in individual life. Preaching without practicing is not respected.
- To work for the love of work and not for the love of money!

---

[17] Pradnya Jere & Y. S. Lele (2003), Dharmavidhinchya Antarangat, Sanskrit Sanskriti Sanshodhika, pg 37

Sadhguru[18] states, there are three occupations that should not be commercialized, namely education, health, and spirituality. He states, when they are commercialized, it marks the beginning of a downfall[19].

In my opinion, it is very valid to charge fees for educational/ religious/spiritual/ healthcare services. Being subject matter experts, professionals deserve to be valued for the knowledge and expertise they carry. Earning livelihood of course is an important element. But at the same time, these work areas are different from pure trade. They touch our existence, our inner consciousness. Hence having transparent pricing, following non-discrimination, and passion for the work, are the subtle elements one would expect from these professionals.

*****

---

[18] Wikipedia The Free Encyclopedia, Sadhguru, https://en.wikipedia.org/wiki/Sadhguru.

[19] Sadhguru (2021), Life and Death in One Breath, Jaico Publishing House, pg 151.

WHEN CAN ONE PERFORM VBS?

The question 'When' has different dimensions as below:

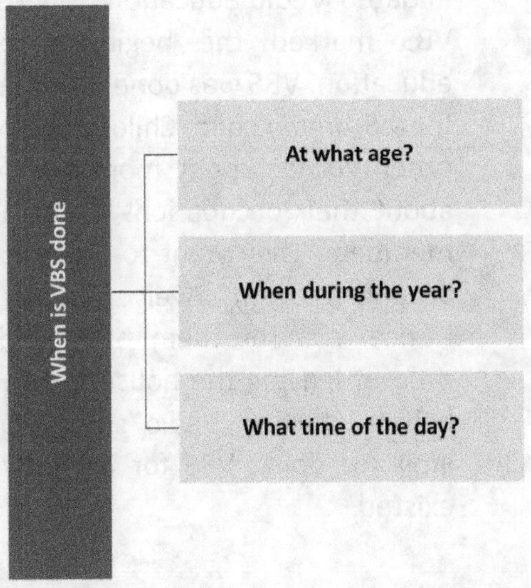

1.   **At what age?**

As we understood earlier, a **child's physical and mental readiness** was a very important aspect to decide when VBS should be planned.   Physical readiness was seen when the child was able to take care of his basic needs like personal hygiene, food, movement and communication.

A rough age range for performing VBS was between 5 to 24 years. The age for VBS was also dependent on the child's *Varna.* For a child of *Brahmin Varna,* the father or other family member often initiated Vedic education in-house. Since VBS marked the beginning of Vedic education, VBS was done at an earlier age for a *Brahmin* child. Children belonging to other *Varnas* spent more time learning about their occupations from the family members. They went to *Gurukulam* later around eleven/ twelve years of age. Hence VBS for them happened at the time of leaving the house for *Gurukulam* before starting Vedic study. An upper limit for doing VBS for each *Varna* also existed.

2.   **When during the year?**

Specific *Ritus/* months were suggested as the ideal time frame to perform VBS for specific *Varnas.* This was based on the environmental conditions and the kind of work one is involved in. The thought behind this was that the weather conditions should not be too harsh at that time and VBS can be performed in full spirit.

In general, a period of five months, from the month of *Magh to Jyeshtha* month was considered favorable.

3. **When during the day**

VBS being an important *Sanskaar,* needed a good amount of planning, especially since the child would leave the house for the *Gurukulam.* An auspicious day and time would be planned for VBS in consultation with a learned astrologer. VBS mostly is done in the first half of the day.

***

WHAT IS THE FLOW OF VBS?

Having understood the What, Why, When of VBS, let us move on to the next question- How?

VBS like any other *Sanskaars* has a set of procedures enlisted. These processes are bound to have variations based on geography, language, *Purohit*, background, culture etc., and are presented as a rough guide here. Yes, some of them need to be re-relooked/ modified/ omitted based on the current situation and needs which we would evaluate further in the upcoming sections.

1. ***Nandi and Devpratishtha*** (नंदी, देवप्रतिष्ठा):

   This is a preparatory step before the actual *Sanskaar*. In this step, the family pays remembrance to the ancestors through the *Nandi Pooja.* During *Devpratishtha,* the family worships *Ganpati,* and other deities praying for a smooth and successful completion of VBS. The night prior to VBS, the child applies turmeric and is supposed to observe *Maun* (silence) to prepare the body and mind for the upcoming big event which is looked at as a second birth.

2. *Chaul* (चौल): This process involves shaving the child's hair. Not entirely, but keeping hair in the center of the head. Symbolism is a big part of Hinduism. This peculiar way of shaving the head was one of the important symbols to identify an *Arya*[20] (Literal meaning- the one who stands for the truth).

Hair is a prominent element in the external beauty of a person. The child should be fully focused on education and not waste time on hair styling and maintenance. Hence this process held an important place in the rituals. It is also believed that the hair that is maintained in the center, also protects the pituitary gland.

3. **Bath:** After shaving the hair, the child is given a bath. It was looked at as a purifying activity

---

[20] Michel Danimo (Third Edition 2011), The Invasion That Never Was, Vivekananda Kendra Prakashan Trust, pg 20

for the body and mind. Bathing also held an important place then, in day-to-day life.

4. **_Matrubhojan_ (मातृभोजन):** This was the last meal that was fed by the mother to the child as a शिशु until she sees him next which was generally after a decade and as a totally transformed human being. The mother is unsure on one hand, will my child be fine without me? and full of aspirations on the other hand, just by thinking how amazing the child is going to turn out. She trusts the process. Both, the child and mother embrace this bittersweet moment with their favorite food, in the company of 8 other _Brahmacharis (Those currently in the BrahmacharyaAshram)._ The _Brahmacharis_ stood as an example, inspiration, and support and provided strength to the duo with their presence. Family and close friends are also invited to this meal.

5. **_Mangalashtake_ (मंगलाष्टके):** This step has three elements.

First: The *Antarpat* (अंतरपाट), a cloth that is held between the child and father. This symbolizes the messages:

- While the cloth is held between us, let my presence not distract you from soaking in the powerful *Mantras* and *Mangalashtakas.*
- Attachment through detachment.
- Even if you don't see us in the coming years, focus on your path and progress. Our blessings are with you always.

Second: *Akshata* (अक्षता). *Akshata* are rice grains, which play an important role in all *Hindu* rituals. It is simply an accepted symbolic medium to communicate blessings and wishes to the subject. The literal meaning of *Akshata* is something that has no end, which is a source of unending power and blessings.

Third: *Mangalashtake.* The important life messages delivered in a song form. The songs convey mainly two messages- one is to provide a glimpse of

BrahmacharyaAshram to the child and to provide guidance on how to lead this phase happily and successfully.

6. ***Mekhala-Kaupin*** (मेखला – कौपिन): *Mekhala* is a thread that is tied around the child's waist, again a symbolic remembrance for the child to not deviate from his goals and to stay focused. This can be better explained using a Hindi phrase 'आगे के पढ़ाव के लिए कमर कस लो'. *Kaupin* is a kind of innerwear given to the child, again with a message that the child now has to be bound by social etiquette and needs to maintain social decorum. Another strong message here is to have control over the senses and not let the mind wander away from the goal of education.

7. ***Ajin*** (अजनि): The child was given a blanket made out of deer skin to keep him warm in harsh weather. Thus, all children in the *Gurukulam* would have deer skin (or other available leather) blankets. The practice of symbolically giving the child a deer skin fabric still continues in some places (well now they offer artificial ones though).

8. ***Fire Worship:*** Performing fire worship is an integral part of various rituals. It is also a part of VBS and has symbolic meanings attached to it. The sacred fire symbolizes life and light. The verses chanted during fire worship are full of educational significance. The child symbolically addressing the sacred fire "O *Agni,* the glorious one, bring me glory. May I become the preserver of the treasures of *Vedas*[21]" Fire worship in a way also symbolizes sacrifice of old ways and embracing the new ones.

9. ***Yagyopavit*** (यज्ञोपावति): The literal meaning of *Yagyopavit* is the one that has emerged from fire worship (*Yagya)*. It is also called as *Janve (*जानवे). It is a cotton thread that is given to the child during VBS. *Janve* is a union of three stands of cotton threads. *Janve* is expected to be worn all through life. It is a symbolic representation, of a person who has attained द्वजित्व (Second birth)

---

[21] Rajbali Pandey (2018), Hindu Samskaras; Socio-Religious Study of the Hindu Sacraments, Motilal Banarasidas Publishers Pvt. Ltd, pg 138

through VBS. Another important symbol that represented the *Arya.*

Like how the uniform reminds a person of where he belongs, and what his rights and duties are, the thread acts like a reminder of the vows taken during VBS. Various interpretations of the significance of this thread are as below. How one looks at it or in how many ways one looks at it can be very different:

- It symbolizes the ways that lead us to the ultimate source of energy, The Creator.
- The three threads symbolize *Brahma, Vishnu,* and *Mahesh.* The Creator, the one who maintains, and the Destroyer.
- A symbol of all the rigorous efforts taken by the person during *Brahmhacharya.*
- A symbolic protective layer that is strengthened by *Gayatri Mantra.*
- A reminder of responsibilities one has towards the family, society, and nation.
- Right to perform *Yagya.*

It is worn from the left shoulder, diagonally running to the right side. It is advised to replace this thread each year (as it gets worn out) during the month of *Shravan.* Evidence from *Ramayana* points out that this thread was not just specific to males but even females wore it[22].

10. ***Gayatri Mantra*** (गायत्री मंत्र): *Gayatri mantra*, is considered a very powerful *Mantra*, the *mantra* that helps sharpen one's intellect. The child is taught *Gayatri Mantra* during VBS. The *Mantra* is about *Savitri-* the Sun. The message is simple but strong:

"Oh Sun, who is the source of inspiration for the entire universe, you are strong and radiant and we meditate on you. May you enlighten us and stimulate our intellect to carry on our work".

Various studies substantiate that chanting of *Gayatri Mantra* brings a lot of positive changes in one's life[23][24][25]. *Gayatri Mantra*

---

[22] Rashtra Sevika Samiti (2011), Upanayan Sanskaar, Shodh va Bodh. pg 113

[23] Rajeev, Gayatri Mantra – Meaning, Significance and Benefits, https://vedicfeed.com/gayatri-mantra-meaning-significance-and-benefits/.

[24] Pradhan B, Derle SG (2012). Comparison of the effect of Gayatri Mantra and Poem Chanting on Digit Letter

teaching and chanting is one of the important steps in VBS. During the GES, children were conditioned to look up to the Sun and the *Vedas* as their mother, and *Guru* as their father. Hence chanting *Gayatri Mantra* also became a connection time, meditating on the symbolic mother figure, which brought a lot of peace to the children.

A school of thought argues against chanting of Gayatri Mantra by females, stating that it has a negative effect on women's reproductive system[26]. However, on enquiring with some women who have undergone VBS, no complaints of this nature have come across.

Substitution Task. Anc Sci Life; 32(2):89-92. doi:10.4103/0257-7941.118540. PMID: 24167333; PMCID: PMC3807963.

[25] K. A. Manoj Narayanan, N. Venugopalan (2018). Effect of Gayatri mantra chanting on cognitive functions in school children. Int J Pediatr Res;5(3):113-115. doi:10.17511/ijpr.2018.3.03

[26] Sinu Joseph (2017), Should Women Chant The Gayatri Mantra? [online] https://mythrispeaks.wordpress.com/2017/03/08/should-women-chant-the-gayatri-mantra/.

11. *Danda* (**दंड**): Self-defense was an important part of education in those times. During VBS, the child was presented with a stick, the *Danda*. Education happened mostly in *Gurukulams*, forest universities, and learning centers away from civilizations. Knowing how and when to use the stick was a crucial life skill for self-protection. It also taught, one should not mindlessly use the tools available, but to the extent need be. Mythology shows us, how the Gods and Goddesses had their own choice of weapons, which they used to destroy evil forces. The child is presented with the same teachings. To use the tool when needed and for the right cause.

12. *Bramhacharya* (**ब्रह्मचर्य**): It is the process where the child is acquainted with the *Vratas* (vows) as elaborated in the next section.

13. *Bhikshawal* (**भिक्षावळ**): *Bhiksha* was a prevalent social system in the past. The

students studying in the *Gurukulams* were required to visit a minimum of 5 houses, requesting (not begging) for food/ food supplies. Yes, this was not begging- it was a beautiful system in place then, where students could rightfully ask for *Bhiksha*. Whatever was collected, was handed over to the *Guru*. Food was then prepared, shared with all, and eaten together. There are some beautiful takeaways from this system:

- The student learns to **share** food, to accumulate what he has got in the common pool (no matter how tempting some food is), and instead of self-enjoyment (giving up the feeling of Me, I) enjoy with everyone. To accept whatever he gets with modesty and gratitude. Can you imagine any student who is a part of this system being a 'fussy'/ 'picky' eater? Likes dislikes, and even having preferences is natural, but accepting what comes in one's plate with grace is what culture teaches.

- Looking at the social angle, it was an accepted norm for people in the other 'Ashramas' mainly those in

Grihasthashram to support students by offering food. As the students graduated and later entered *Grihasthashram,* switching roles was natural, effortless, and reciprocatory.

- This practice was a medium for the students to stay connected with people, identify societal problems, and absorb the socio-economic and political currents.

- From a financial perspective, this system took off the load of managing food finance from *Gurukulams.* This in turn helped them to completely focus on the core objective, which was education.

Today, however, this ritual is a part of VBS simply as an act of play.

Fun Fact: The fifth incarnation of Lord Vishnu- The Vamanavatar also denotes Batu (बटु) the Brahmin who is asking Bhiksha.

14. ***Poshakh*** (पोषाख): During VBS and further in the *Gurukulams,* the child was taught (and would wear) a type of clothing, which is

white (to help against heat), simple (easy to wear), made out of cotton (suitable for Indian climate) and convenient (to perform day to day activities with ease). It acted like a uniform. The focus behind this was minimalism and convenience.

15. *Sandhya* (संध्या): The child is taught and instructed to perform *'Sandhya'* every day at sunrise and sunset like morning rituals and bedtime routine! It includes a set of activities like daily prayers to the Sun and fire, doing Yoga, meditation, *pranayama,* chanting *Gayatri Mantra etc.* This practice has its own reason and scientific basis behind it. Let us understand it through an example:

Have you observed how the preparation for a regular school day starts from the previous evening, for a child?

Complete the homework, pack the school bag, keep the uniform ready, and sleep on time. In the morning it's a different rush altogether! Wake up on time, do morning rituals, pack tiffin, get ready, eat breakfast, rush on time to get the school bus, and so on. This is nothing but the mind, body, and soul working toward an objective.

Sandhya is a form of preparatory ritual for the child but on a spiritual, and psychological level. The practice aims at getting the child to stay focused, prepare for the tasks to be done, express gratitude, and so on. A method of reflection.

The actual prescribed steps for performing *Sandhya* will vary based on location/ culture/ *Guru* etc. But the crux of this step is to get into a daily habit of preparing the mind, body, and soul for the task at hand.

16. *Chitrahuti* (चतिराहुती): The child is taught to pay **gratitude** towards food, before eating it. There are a few *Mantras* prescribed before eating food, which one has to chant. The idea is not just to be thankful for the food, but for everyone and everything that makes it possible for the food to reach us. The prayer

also expresses gratitude for the energy within that turns the food a part of our body.

17. **_VedArambha_** (*वेदारंभ*): This is the 12th *Sanskaar.* This was done after VBS, in the *Gurukulam,* before formally commencing the study of *Vedas.* This step mainly involved fire worship. Today, this *Sanskaar* is included during VBS itself.

In an overview of the various steps involved, we generally see a few common messages that pop out of the rituals and *Sanatana Dharma* at large. Expressing gratitude, working towards reaching the ultimate goal of life which is *Moksha* (Union with the Creator and liberation from the cycle of life and death), the act of giving and helping others, working on developing good qualities and giving away the not-so-right ones, and being righteous.

***

WHAT ARE THE *VRATAS* PRESCRIBED IN VBS?

Before the child left for education, the child was familiarized with certain rules/ rhythms to be followed. Since these were a societal norm, a way of life in itself, these *vratas* were quite obvious then and didn't look like a big deal. They were an integral part of the culture. During VBS, the child formally would accept these *vratas*.

These *vratas* are aimed at helping an individual reach intellectual and spiritual goals. These *vratas* were designed to aid the overall development of the child including education, physical fitness, interpersonal relationships, spiritual growth, mental wellness, social behavior etc. These *Vratas* also helped inculcate the meaning of '*Brahmacharya*' which means self-control and self- discipline[27]. *Brahmacharya*

---

[27] Swati Chanchani & Rajiv Chanchani (2021), Yoga for Children, CBS Publishers & Distributors, pg 20.

carries the spirit — Everything belongs to the Supreme Energy.

These *Vratas* were expected to be followed by the child until he finished his education (until the graduation ceremony, which is the *Samavartana Sanskaar*) and some continued lifelong. The different things prescribed to be followed were as below:

1. **Self-Cleanliness**: Taking care of one's elimination, bath, and personal hygiene. Washing hands and feet after elimination and also before eating.

2. To perform daily **Sandhya:** This is with an intention of staying focused, building discipline, and mental stability.

3. **Not to sleep** during the day.

4. To be an **obedient student**, and to soak in all the knowledge the *Guru* has to impart. But if the *Guru* acts or instructs to

act in a way that is not rightful, the student should question and stick to the path of righteousness.

5.   *Bhiksha*: This was a part of the daily rituals for the students. It taught the message: let food not be a reason for you to get distracted from your learning journey, accept what you get with gratitude, share what you get amongst all with love, and eat it with satisfaction.

6.   To stay away from **sensory pleasures**: A student is expected to stay away from sensory pleasures. One should use the sensory organs- ear, nose, eyes, skin, and tongue for the purpose of learning or doing something constructive. One should not exploit the senses with sensory objects, which at first are pleasurable but in the end are the cause of negative emotions like sorrow, greed, lust, and so on[28]. One needs to be aware

---

[28] Swami Tejomayananda (2022), Dharma Shastra, Way to

that he is the one who needs to control the senses and not otherwise.

7. **Agni Pooja:** Being engaged in fire worship by offering *Samidha* (wood offerings) to the fire. It was observed that concentration and learning after this activity was more effective. This, however, is not practical in today's mainstream education system. However, *Agni* and light, in general carry huge importance in *Sanatana Dharma* and are an integral part of rituals, and day-to-day life[29].

8. Other **behavior-related** advice: Avoid too much of anything. Stay away from greed, pride, fear, sorrow, and anger. Eat simple, *satvic* food which is juicy and wholesome which can give health and happiness. Avoid food which is too spicy,

---

Peace, Prosperity and Purity, Chinmaya Prakashan, pg 10.

[29] Swami Vimalananda & Radhika Krishnakumar (2019), In Indian Culture, Why Do We, Chinmaya Prakashan, pg 1.

too salty, too pungent, too bitter, dry or burning which can cause disease and distress[30]. And not to consume intoxicating substances.

***

[30] A.C. Bhaktivedanta Swami Prabhupada (1972), Bhagavad Gita as it is, The Bhaktivedanta Book Trust, pg 680.

PART 2: THE BRAIN-TEASERS

IS VBS RELEVANT TODAY?

It is important to evaluate relevance of VBS in light of the contemporary social structure. To evaluate if VBS is still relevant today, it is important to revisit what objectives does VBS fulfill? If we go back to the first section, we understand that VBS serves the three objectives:

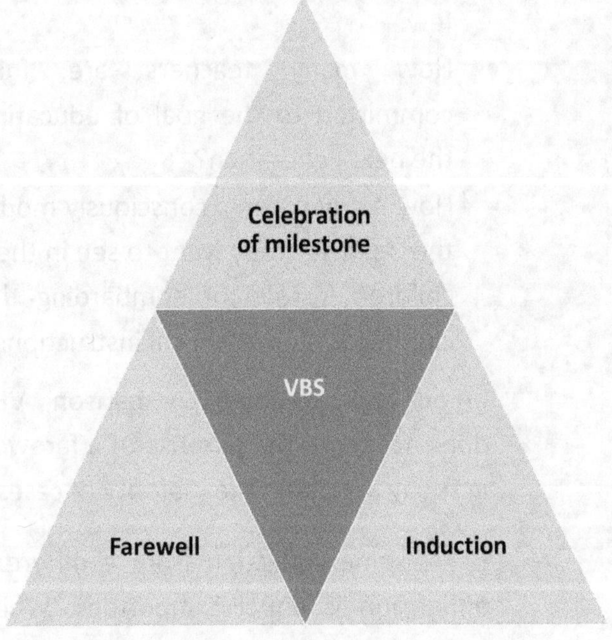

1. Farewell
2. Celebration of milestone
3. Induction for the next stage of life

Let's analyze each of these!

1. **Farewell:** During GES, the child left house after VBS for a decade or more. Today:

    - What percentage of children go to *Gurukulams*? **Very few.**
    - What percentage of children are admitted to boarding schools? Very few.
    - How many teachers are fully committed to the goal of educating the next generation?
    - How many parents consciously model the behavior they want to see in their children instead of bombarding the children with theoretical instructions?

    In an apple-to-apple comparison, VBS does not serve the purpose of a farewell in today's times in the majority of cases.

    Here, some reflection from a different dimension is equally important. While today the children are staying with their parents, how many children going to school get to spend decent quality time with the primary caregivers? A child above seven years typically spends about six hours in school, a couple of hours doing homework, a few hours in classes and some time in play. The day ends with a rush to get ready for school the next day. Moreover, today, parents are busier, families are smaller, time is a major limiting factor, needs and preferences of people have changed. All this makes parent-child interaction very very limited.

The child needs to 'study' becomes the focus, and is excused even from daily chores. The child focuses purely on academics in order to get 'educated'. Sadly, this not only limits the child's learning, but also negatively impacts the child's social interactions, personality development, physical fitness, spiritual growth, when all this rather should be blossoming through real education.

So, while the child does not 'leave' the house physically, has the family and house become merely a place to stay, **a**

lodging and boarding facility? is something one needs to evaluate and work upon. Today we see children distancing from caregivers not physically but emotionally, from very young ages. We see children facing mental health issues. All this puts a question mark on the current education and social system. It magnifies the need for increased parental intervention from yearly years for the holistic development of the child.

Today, let VBS be the **farewell to the 'authoritative parent' within!** Let VBS be the reason for caregivers to embrace the (new) mentor selves. Bid farewell, not to the child, but to our false egos and superiority complexes.

Suggestions:

- Review how primary caregivers can include some quality time with the child each day.
- A family circle time on a daily/ weekly basis can be introduced, where the

family comes together to plan their day/ week, share their feelings.

- Open discussions and debates on the systems that existed before, on systems that exist in different cultures and countries. Talk about the historical incidents and their impact on the culture. Get the child's view on the same to co-create ideas that can bring value to the family.
- Segregate individual work timings. So that, when the child is at home, at least one grown-up is available for engagement if needed.

2. **Celebration of milestone:** VBS marked the progression of a child from *ShishuAwastha* to *BrahmacharyaAshram-* the phase focusing on education and skill building.

If you have a preschooler, you would know, there is something different about this age group. A difference in behavior becomes evident around 7 years of age. A different level of confidence and independence reflects in the child. The child does not need parental care and guidance in most scenarios.

This shift from Level 0 (*ShishuAwastha)* to Level 1, also is reflected in day–to–day activities such as:

- Personal care: Being able to take care of own input and output without needing much help from grown-ups.
- Power of discretion: To be able to distinguish between right, wrong, good, and bad.
- Physical independence: To be able to move in known places confidently and independently.
- Wanting someone as a mentor, but not wanting to be totally dependent on the mentor either. A strong urge to explore and discover the world around.

There is also a famous Sanskrit verse on how the parenting equation changes with the progression of age of the child. The meaning of the verse is- provide them with unrestricted love for the first five years, discipline them next ten years and as they reach sixteen, treat them as your friend. Now these years 5, 16 are indicative and would vary from child to child. And we would look at 'discipline' more from a role modeling/ mentoring angle today.

लालयेत् पंच वर्षाणि दिश वर्षाणि ताड्येत्।

प्राप्ते षोड्शे वर्षे पुत्रे मित्रिवदाचरेत्॥

Most of the religions, most of the educational philosophies, tribes, and communities have specific ritual/ milestone nomenclature to denote this new phase of a child stepping out of *ShishuAwastha*

- Mainstream education – 'primary schooling'
- Montessori method- 'Elementary child'/ 'Second plane of life'
- Waldorf method- 'Middle childhood'

- Sanatana Dharma- BrahmacharyaAshram marked by VBS
- Parsis- 'Navjote'
- Christianity- 'Baptism'
- Muslim- 'Khatna'
- Buddhism- 'Pabbajja'/ 'Upasampada'
- Sikhism- 'Amrit ceremony'
- Some tribes- test of endurance, mutation etc.

Some of these have purely educational flavors, some purely religious and some combine both. The essence of these being initiation of a child in the community, making the child aware of the rights and duties attached to being in the particular community. The perfect example that combines both religious and educational intentions is VBS. Thus VBS, even today, fulfills the objective of being that tool for celebration. Celebrating the milestone of a child's promotion to the next level. Celebrating the beginning of some serious learning and skill-building!

"Why should we not look at birthday as a reason to celebrate the milestone? one may argue, "We anyways do that yearly". A birthday, in essence, is merely a celebration. Meaningful discussions, and mental preparation to consciously induct the child for the next level of life lack here. The beauty of VBS is the culmination of multiple intentions and actions at the same time. Maybe one can merge the two and plan VBS on the child's birthday itself!

Suggestions:

- Use various resources to talk to the child about life's progressions from early childhood.
- Read your child to find out his interests and to plan resources for skill building accordingly.
- Caregivers can use age-appropriate resources for child sexuality education31. This helps children to

---

[31] Federal Center for Health Education, Sexuality Education Policy Brief No. 1 [online]

understand their bodies and boundaries.

- If the caregivers do not opt for VBS, the caregivers should still consciously weave in the missing pieces to bring in awareness to the child about the rollover to the next stage of life and what it entails.

3. **Induction:** During VBS, the child was inducted to the next level of *BrahmacharyAshram* by way of the vows. In the GES the vows were nothing but a societal norm. They did not seem burdensome, irrelevant or illogical.

Today, when the child is asked to take the same vows as were applicable then, the child is bound to experience unpleasantness and reluctance to follow any of those. Especially, since he does not see these vows being followed by majority of the people around him.

---

https://www.euro.who.int/__data/assets/pdf_file/0008/3
79043/Sexuality_education_Policy_brief_No_1.pdf.

As a corollary, what is seen around, even if not right, gets normalized. "During VBS I was told not to drink alcohol, but who cares, I see my friends and family doing it, that's the norm, that's what modern people do!". That what is common gets normalized.

A change can be seen only when the child, by will, signs up for something. The fire within leading him to do or abstain from doing something is what we have to ignite as caregivers and *Gurus*. Carrot – stick approach is a passe.

So what do we need to do to make VBS meet this objective of induction? Refer to the upcoming section on how to co-design the vows, along with the below suggestions:

- Have open discussions within the family and discuss the vows that were taken then. Take everyone's views on the same in terms of their relevance today.
- Curate vows which are practically feasible and sustainable.

- Have some short-term vows and some long-term vows. Just like the yearly appraisal system at workplaces, develop a system to evaluate/ modify these vows on a timely basis as may be needed.

Summary: Does VBS fulfill its objectives today?

Objective	Status	Comments
Farewell	✓	Farewell - not for the child but to authoritative parenting styles
Celebration of milestone	✓	In the presence of child's well-wishers and family
Induction	✓	Through meaningful vows

When there is clarity on the 'Why' of VBS and the underlying sentiment of VBS, one can still weave in the other secondary social elements. Like the scale of the celebration, food, dressing up, and all things linked with 'event management. These aspects do have their place in the scheme of things but to what extent is something that varies from family to family. But if the very awareness about the 'Why' of the *Sanskaar* is missing, everything else turns superficial!

The essence of VBS is to celebrate the child's readiness to transition to the next level and to help the child gear up for the next stage of life. The preparatory stage of VBS itself opens up beautiful possibilities within a family to talk about a multitude of topics related to life. VBS becomes the reason for seeking, questioning, and finding answers to many questions that follow later. VBS has the potential to transform a family.

Thus, VBS can be performed for a child irrespective of:

- Where and how the child is studying
- Is the child living in a boarding school, his own house, or growing up in an orphanage
- Which caste does the child belong to

- Gender of the child, etc.

and be made meaningful and relevant in today's times by aware and involved caregivers.

Now, some people might opt for VBS purely from a **religious** point of view, or to merely do their bit to **carry forward the traditions**. Here, it serves a very limited purpose. Nonetheless, if that is what one wants, VBS becomes relevant for this section of society too.

***

WILL MY CHILD NOT SUCCEED IF WE OPT OUT OF VBS?

Short answer: **No! Success is not dependent on VBS**, VBS is just a tool to increase the probability of success.

Every action we take is done with a set of expected outcomes in mind. And this is driven by our belief system. Belief, not related to God or religion as such but belief in the process with the hope of a favorable outcome.

Success is a subjective term in itself. And the fact is, no matter what you do, it is not going to guarantee success for someone else! So, the best you can do is to do what you feel is right. It will increase the probability of success, the way you see it from your lens.

A farmer puts in a lot of hard work before he gets the yield. He plows, de-weeds, sows the seeds carefully, water regularly, install a scarecrow, manage infestation etc. Does that guarantee him a great yield always? No, all this just increases his probability to get a good yield. On the contrary, thousands of trees flourish in the wild without having anyone to tend to them while millions of seeds don't even get to sprout.

Similarly, VBS is **not the passport to success** in life. But at the same time, VBS when done thoughtfully, has a great probability of leaving a positive mark on the child and the way he grows up. VBS is like a curated process to 'transplant' the sapling from the nursery into the ground. Here caregivers, like the farmer, prepare the ground for the sapling to grow. The sapling will ultimately find its way!

Let us look at some traditions, and various rituals in society:

1. Naming ceremony: The child carries his name with pride all through life irrespective of the scale and nature of the naming ceremony.

2. Birthday: People across the globe celebrate birthdays, and the 'how' varies from family to family. How one celebrates does not determine if the child will grow better than another. At the same time not having a celebration does not hinder growth either. But the 'how' does have subtle impact on the child in different forms!

3. Marriage: Same goes for marriages. Whether one gets married in the court or in the presence of close family or a crowd, what sustains a marriage is not the form in which the union got a nod, but how well the couple understands and blends with the spirit of the union. Having said that, when some social element is attached to this union, it does add an additional sense of responsibility in the relationship, some extra tinge of compulsive obedience (right or not is a different discussion altogether).

4. Death: Various rituals to be performed on the death of a person have been prescribed in each religion. Does someone's soul attain *Moksha* if the final

rites were performed in the utmost 'original' form? Does something go wrong because no last rites were performed at all[32]? It all drills down to **beliefs** after all!

5. New Year Party: As a norm, people across the world celebrate the end and beginning of a new calendar year in a variety of ways. But the truth is whether the humans dance away, drink, sleep off, watch television, or cut a cake, the Earth will continue to revolve and rotate and keep doing its *Karma!*

6. Many more examples like these- cracking coconut on buying a new vehicle, housewarming (*Vastushanti*), doing or not doing certain things on particular days of the week, etc.

All these actions spring out of belief systems. Thus, the answer to this question can be aptly

---

[32] Sarala Nirmal (2021), Salutations to You! Oh Death!, Mythree Samprathishtaana.

summarized through this verse from the *Bhagwad Gita:*

कर्मण्येवाधिकारस्ते मा फलेषु कदाचन।

मा कर्मफलहेतुर्भूर्मा ते सङ्गोऽस्त्वकर्मणि॥ २-४७

Do what you need to do, without being attached to the result. If you see merit in doing VBS, take it forward. But don't do VBS thinking it will guarantee success for your child.

***

WHAT ARE THE OTHER DIMENSIONS WHICH PRIMARY CAREGIVERS SHOULD BE AWARE OF?

Before the child shows readiness for VBS, it is important for the primary caregivers of the child to have an understanding of other dimensions linked with VBS. With changing times, and changing systems, keeping a voice inside that questions, reviews, and modifies things is needed. Else things become stagnant and obsolete! Evaluation of these varied dimensions will help prepare the caregivers before they start preparing the child!

1. **Holistic Development:** As soon as the child turns two, caregivers start looking for different programs, food items, medicines, etc., to ensure their child becomes intelligent, smart, independent and what not! Caregivers already have a wishlist and set of expectations from the child in most cases. Ultimately, everyone wants the next generation to be

independent, intelligent as well as sensitive. But no one knows how or which is the right way.

Like how a marble in mud shines when cleaned off, like how a sapling grows into a tree when taken care of in the initial days, like how the cycle runs better when the chain is cleaned regularly- *the Sanskaars* do the job of **'maintenance and upliftment'**. VBS is an instrument which can bring a positive change in the child's life. The preparatory phase for VBS and the *vratas* one continues to follow, help in a child's holistic development.

While the *Sanskaars* have a religious angle, one cannot dismiss other dimensions attached to them.

2. **Religious angle**: For a household that believes in the traditional ways of doing things, VBS carries a lot of importance. VBS is still considered as one of the most

significant *Sanskaars* out of the 16. Even in such cases, where the underlying reason for performing VBS is purely religious, or to carry forward the tradition, the key is to ensure the child's opinions and views are respected. The child should be involved in the whole process and not treated merely as a 'Subject'. If not, the child can develop negative feelings for any and all religious/ spiritual activities.

3. **Impact on the child:** A child celebrates his birthday, and suddenly as a switch is turned on, behaves like a grown-up kid. This is manifested through his language and actions. Similarly, VBS helps the child look forward to the new stage of life positively and proactively. The preparation stage for VBS sets the stage for reflection and acts as a roadmap for the child. It helps the child to accept and embrace the promotion from *ShishuAwastha* to *BrahmacharyaAshram*.

Just as we feel excited during the summer holidays when we buy new books for the next grade, new uniforms, and new school bags, VBS prepares the child for the upcoming stage of life. Can you connect the dots here?

4. **A milestone:** Be it small things like doing a *pooja* on buying a new vehicle, clapping with joy when the child takes his first steps, printing 'something/ anything' just because you got a new printer? VBS is a way of celebration, where friends and family gather to celebrate this big milestone. When the child is fully aware of the 'Why' and 'How' and 'What' of VBS, the child participates in the process with enthusiasm.

5. **The Social Element:** A couple that gets married in front of hundreds of people, carries that extra social obligation of sticking to the vows versus a 'Live-in' couple? To a certain extent, yes. We cannot deny the fact that social elements

do carry weight and influence decisions. Whether this is the right thing or not is a separate discussion.

Similarly, by making VBS a grand affair and inviting the 'who's who', can put undue pressure on the child. It also wrongly fuels the message that social validations are important. This is not what VBS is for. Hence keeping VBS limited to **real well-wishers** of the child is more meaningful.

6. **Education System:** Today we see a wide spectrum of methods of education. Right from the mainstream education system to open learning. The mainstream education system focuses on authoritative teaching styles. It focuses mainly on 'delivering information' to crack the exams.

Whereas open learning believes in self-directed learning driven by own desires.

It is a learning experience without the boundaries of a curriculum.

Within these two, lie other learning possibilities like alternative education systems, homeschooling, etc. But we must acknowledge, **no system is perfect**!

Likewise, we cannot say 'Old is always Gold!' *GES* too would have its own flaws. A few apparent ones to note would be the distancing from family and lack of communication with them.

But is it possible to have a **new *GES*,** where we handpick the pros of various educational systems? New GES where modern education is clubbed with Vedic wisdom? Where the child is not expected to just score marks. Where the focus is on sharpening one's intellect, physical well-being, vedic knowledge, psychological well-being, spiritual awareness, hands-on learning, and understanding of duties towards the nation?

All this while being an **independent as a learner**[33] to learn based on one's interests and abilities, under the guidance of able *Gurus*. It would be a beautiful culmination of western and Indian education as also envisaged by Swami Vivekananda! Possibly a residential learning system after the child reaches a certain age and when ready, with healthy channels to connect and communicate with the family. Fortunately, we do see efforts by many institutions on these lines today! Let us hope the perceived **new GES** turns out to be the **new normal** in the coming decades!

We do see a ray of hope through the **New Education Policy** too. When implemented in the true spirit it will

---

[33] ChinamayaChannel, Should The Teacher Carry You To Heaven? - Lift Yourself! - Chapter 6 Verse 5 [online] https://youtu.be/b8iynPEW3oU.

surely help in the overall child development.

7. **The teacher–student relationship:** A right *Guru* has the potential to turn the most boring subject interesting for a child. On the contrary, a teacher who is just doing the 'job' of delivering information can turn the student off from the subject he loves! A *Guru* is that instrument which helps the child unlock his own potentials and to uncover the knowledge within[34]. Yes, having a right *Guru* can change things magically. And it is indeed a blessing to find the right *Guru*.

In GES, *Guru* was a father figure as well as a mentor who dedicated his life to educating young children. And the student (*Vidyarthi)* was a sincere seeker.

---

[34] Vedanta Kesari, Education: A Ramakrishna-Vivekananda Perspective [online] https://www.swamivivekananda.guru/2021/05/12/education-a-ramakrishna-vivekananda-perspective/.

Vidyarthi (विद्यार्थी), literally translates to the one who is begging for knowledge.

Today, our kids have multiple *Gurus* (teacher is the right word). Teachers do their job by ensuring the syllabus is completed within time. The focus is mainly to score in exams and move to the next class. Learning has turned into a mere give-and-take. Fire in the belly to learn is not the driver for education in most cases. And "Begging for knowledge? Excuse me who does that" is the attitude!

Considering the current situation, below are some reflective questions:

- Can the primary caregivers step up as Gurus and be less of 'Parents'?
- Can we walk the talk with the child, so that the child doesn't feel demotivated?
- Are we able to read our child and his interests?

- Do we have the right resources to support the child's interests?
- Are we able to choose the right school/ teacher for our child that resonates with our principles and the child's interests?
- Can we build an environment at home that teaches a child to be truly independent, and interdependent when need be?
- Can we inculcate the right values that reflect through our own behavior?
- Do we look at schools as a medium to conveniently offload the responsibility of a child's education in lieu of money?
- How involved are we in the child's learning process?

8. **Life Progression and family conflicts:** We often praise the westerners thinking "How independent are the kids in the West, they step out 'into the unknown' at 18 years!" When we look at GES, children

mostly were stepping out of homes at the pre-teen stage. Staying away from the comfort of homes and loved ones, and doing things independently while being grounded!

Today when we generally see one or two children per family, the earlier life progression template would work beautifully in modern times. It has the potential to take care of all the issues we face today! But well, it assumes two fundamentals (which today are shaky though): a **strong marriage and new GES**.

Let us look at the below pictorial **example** of life progressions if applied in today's time with the above assumptions. The age range is ofurse indicative.

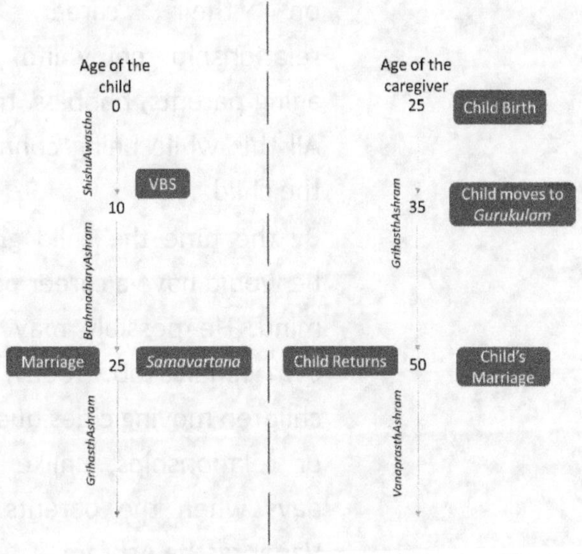

Observations:

- Core parenting that calls for focused efforts spans for about ten years, till the child leaves for new GES after a thoughtfully curated VBS.

- The child in new GES gets access to good quality education. The child spends about 10 - 15 years in this system.

- While the child is in new GES, caregivers get the time to focus

- on their career, mutual relationship, enjoy life, care for aging parents, hobbies, travel etc. All this while being connected to the child.

- By the time the child graduates, he would have a career path in his mind. He possibly may start his own family too. Today, we see children moving cities due to work or relationships, unlike the GES days when the parents left for Vanaprastha Ashram.

- In effect one can observe that the system is designed on 'Attachment through detachment' principles after the child leaves the nest.

And the cycle continues!

'Me time', 'Family time', 'Career time', and 'Retirement time' all can be weaved in life progressions beautifully. This naturally will leave **little scope for *'Tu Tu – Main Main'*.**

9. **Social Decorum and Etiquettes:** When a child is still in *ShishuAwastha* the child knows no rules and is still trying to make sense of things around him. Typically, children in this stage:

- Are not conscious about their clothing,
- Eat randomly from the plates of others,
- Don't mind bathing in open,
- Are in physical proximity of other family members without any inhibition. Sitting on laps, hugging or getting kisses from other family members, etc. is common,
- are not always aligned with the rhythm of the family e.g., wake-up, sleep time, elimination cycles, food times etc.

All these acts are excused, ignored, and not looked at as something unusual or unacceptable. Because the child is still not there yet to understand social etiquette. The child is still absorbing and learning from the environment. But as the child nears the 7-year mark, one can observe the child getting conscious of self, their surroundings, and his behaviors. VBS helps a child with this realization and to shape social behavior.

10. **National Integration and development:** This is a macro-level thought. Imagine the majority of families opting for VBS in the right spirit with the right mental preparation for the child. Imagine all these families who are making changes at a micro level in their households! We would be progressing as a nation with a next-gen that is focusing on real learning, that is aware of innate skills, that is independent yet interdependent, progressive, healthy, mindful, spiritually developed, and intelligent. That would be the time when Bharat would truly be *Atmanirbhar* (Self-sufficient) and no one to question 'अच्छे दिन'!

11. **Non-Discrimination:** It is commonly observed that children face a lot of discrimination amongst themselves on the basis of whether VBS is performed or not. The children who have undergone VBS, claim superiority over those who have not, the children belonging to a particular religion/caste boast about their notional eligibility for VBS.

Shaming and criticizing also happens based on the scale of operations for the *Sanskaar.* Some do it in a magnificent, ceremonial way. Some like to keep it simple and homely. Some also get it done together in *Samudayik Vratabandha Sohola* (VBS done for many children together).

Whether to opt for VBS or not is purely a family decision. At the same time, the scale of VBS is purely a choice made by the family based on their preferences and feasibility. Family decisions and choices should be respected.

As caregivers, we need to actively sow the seeds of equal treatment and non-discrimination in children from the early years and model it in our day-to-day interactions. VBS is a tool, a great tool no doubt. But **not an instrument to demean** anyone.

***

HOW CAN ONE PREPARE A CHILD FOR VBS?

Child's preparedness is a very important element for VBS to be a transformative *Sanskaar* for the child. The preparedness is seen on **two levels: physical and mental**. We have already understood the aspect of physical readiness in the previous sections. But how can one prepare a child mentally? Now, this process is not constrained to someone who believes in VBS.

It drills down to the quality of the environment we are building around the little humans. To pick up values and ways of life. Hence this process is not triggered just at the thought of doing VBS, but begins right from infancy, and is applicable to all! It is an enriching process and opens the doors to many more meaningful conversations on an ongoing basis, as a part of family culture. This is very healthy and often seen as lacking in modern family structures.

How does mental conditioning for a child happen?

A child has three ways in which he makes sense of the world around him.

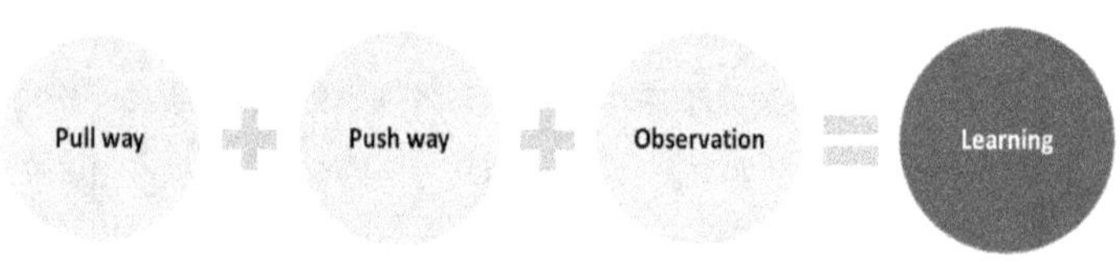

The 'Pull Way': Children from a very young age have plenty of questions to ask about life, why do we do this, why not that, how does this work, etc. It is important we as primary caregivers, always answer them. Answer as truly as we can and in an age-appropriate way. Never lie.

Below are some common questions that children have and their simple answers in a child-friendly way. You can modify the explanations based on the level of understanding of your child.

1.   Who is God?

        We drive a car and decide where it should go. We switch on the fan when it is hot. But there are so many things around us, which seem to happen on their own. How does the wind blow? How do the flowers bloom? Who puts life in the body? How does the sun rise daily and not take a holiday? This, and so many things around us happen without someone making them work!

This energy which is unseen but runs these systems is what people refer to as God! Let us call it **The Creator**. Because the moment we call it God, we try to attach a form to it based on what we know so far. The Creator is that energy, that force that keeps the universe going!

How you perceive it is a personal discovery altogether[35]. Some believe the energy in everything around us is God, some give it a form of an idol, some

---

[35] Swami Vivekananda (2022), The Complete Book of Yoga, FingerPrint Life, pg303.

believe there is just one God and look at some humans as his messengers, etc.

To start with, why not just acknowledge the Creator and try to unfold his identity through your own lens? To understand the Creator, there is no mandate to sign up for any religion too. Be a good human being, that is the best you can do for yourself and society.

2.   What is religion?
        With a new machine, we usually get a user manual. Religion is like a **user manual** that talks about how to make the most of this life. Religion helps us use the body, our mega-machine, in the best possible way to sync in with the purpose of life! Now these 'user manuals' come in different forms, colors, and shapes. Hence, we see different religions around the world. They all ultimately carry the same spirit[36].

---

[36] A.C. Bhaktivedanta Swami Prabhupada (2018), Basics of

So, while one is born into a religion, one can always choose a different religion later in life. One can even choose not to choose any!

However today, in the name of religion, we see a lot of violence, and that is definitely not why the Creator would have made us right? Treating one religion as superior to another is not right. Keeping aside our individual biases, it is important to be tolerant[37] and respect the choices of others. After all, different religions are different forms of user manuals!

3.   What are cultures and traditions?
Culture is all those things that happen around us. The food we eat, the language, clothing, values, norms, symbols, and gestures all are a part of the

---

Bhagwad-Gita, The Bhaktivedanta Book Trust, pg 77.

[37] Ravindra Bodhe (2021), Yoga and Value Education, O. P. Tiwari Kaivalyadham, pg 81.

culture. Like, the saying 'The city of Mumbai never sleeps'! Like in southern India, beautiful rangolis are drawn in front of houses. That's all a part of the culture of that region. Culture carries many flavors and is not just religious.

Whereas tradition are the things done from generation to generation based on certain beliefs. For example, The Reddy family follows a tradition of baking a cake on New Year's Eve.

4.	Each religion has some scriptures, what are they?
Religions are belief systems where important beliefs, dos and don'ts are documented in some form. These are called scriptures.

5.	Is it important to learn?
Learning is a natural process. See how a child is curious to know the world around him and loves exploring! By touching, smelling, tasting, hearing, and by looking around! We learn unknowingly from

people, things, events, and the environment around us. We are born curious and always carry a spark in us to learn and experiment.

Literacy is a different dimension: learning to read, write and communicate. To be educated is to learn and be literate. It is important in today's world, to develop expertise in what you like doing, to earn a living, to enjoy the process, and to be an asset to society.

6. What is Death?

Look at the body as a house rented out by the soul. A house better cared for, well maintained, serves, and functions longer. When the body becomes old or is physically damaged, it is no more suitable to function and the soul has to exit[38]. This is called death. That's why so much stress on taking care of our bodies!

---

[38] ChinamayaChannel, Bhagavad Geeta - Death & Rebirth (Chapter 2 Verse 22) https://www.youtube.com/watch?v=Dy-QLmh_yjY.

*Another way to help children understand death is to involve them in **green waste composting!***

7. Why am I darker than her? Does that mean I am weaker?

   We all have different bodies, body colors and we come in different shapes and sizes. We are all unique. Just like we can have different eye colors like black, brown, blue, grey, etc. our skin tones can vary too. These things do not decide a person's ability. What I more important is the function than the form!

   You will get a lot of resources on subjects like body differences, birth, diversity in family structures, etc. in children's book form. This will help you answer many such questions which children ask.

   It is important to use the correct nomenclatures for the body parts and to not express shame or shyness while *talking about these topics with your children. These talks are **important.***

8. Sense Organs: Like the body helps us perform our actions, the sense organs help us get a sense of the outside world. We smell, touch, see, taste, and hear to understand the world around us. Just like the body, we are meant to use them to perform our *Karma* (work). But if you look closely, the tables have turned. We are conditioned to think that happiness comes from expensive things, happiness comes from buying things. Simple examples, even after a full meal, that ice cream looks yummy, and we end up having a bowl full! It is late in the night, well past bedtime, but can't let go of scrolling the reels! Relatable? Because the 'wanting' never ends, and constant wanting of one thing then another, makes us greedy, irritable, and unhappy.

The 'Push Way': These are the topics that the primary caregivers can introduce suo-moto, without any active inquiry from the child. This is the opportunity where all the family members can share thoughts, discuss, deliberate, and have open conversations on these topics. These topics talk about the belief systems of the religion he is born in. When it comes to *Sanatana Dharma*, you can include the below topics in your conversations. (One can always include talks weaving knowledge about different religions and belief systems)

1.   About Hinduism:

Hinduism is a relatively newer term. Did you know there was no such word as Hindu? It is derived from the word Sindhu[39]. The Sindhu civilization was referred to as the civilization that developed along the banks of the Sindhu River. When the Persians came, they started referring to the civilization as Hindus, since they

---

[39] Sanatan Says, Are We Hindus? by Swami Sampatidasa [online] https://www.youtube.com/shorts/GxfKNfbZHpM.

could not pronounce the word Sindhu. Thus, Hinduism is more to do with geographical identity than a religious system. The Hindus follow *Sanatana Dharma*. It believes in 'One God' with different forms[40].

If you ask me, do not get stuck in the terminologies like Hinduism/ Sanatana Dharma/ Vedic culture, etc. What is important to know is, all these are like a river and her tributaries. They all carry the same water and seek the same thing- knowing and becoming one with the ocean (The Creator).

Sanatana Dharma is not compulsive and offers freedom to choose. To choose what and how one wants to progress in life, how one should seek the Creator, what work one can do, what is good for health so on and so forth. It touches upon

---

[40] Central Chinmaya Mission Trust (2019), Hinduism: Frequently Asked Questions, Chinmaya Prakashan, pg 5.

a multitude of human traits and dimensions and provides a roadmap of how to live a good life.

2. About idol worship:

A common misconception we see about Hinduism is that it is synonymous with idol worship. But idol worship is a medium used to worship the ideals which the idols represent[41]. Just the way a country's flag represents the country, and is not the country by itself, idols represent the qualities of the different Gods and Goddesses and mythological characters. *Sanatana Dharma* believes that there is only One Creator, which is without a concrete form and is present everywhere and in all. All the 'Gods' we see in the temples are different forms of the Creator himself and the idea is to worship the qualities of that respective form.

---

[41] Swami Vimalananda (2019), Hinduism: Frequently Asked Questions, Central Chinmaya Prakashan, pg 36.

3. The Hindu Scriptures*:*

   Sanatana Dharma does not have a specific rule book but has various scriptures where the wisdom is documented. Like *Vedas, Upanishads, Bhagwat Geeta, Puranas,* etc. to name a few. Now you would think, all this is so confusing, how can one understand what *Sanatana Dharma* is trying to tell? No one has so much time or capability to read through all these scriptures! True, but today with access to media, you can easily navigate through this information with some good YouTube channels/ institutions that carry out crash courses/ books/ podcasts and even *Gurus* (mentors) who you feel can help you simplify things.

4. About The Stages of Life:

   Like in the games you play, you have different levels, right? Each level has its own challenges and fun elements. Similarly, a full life, like a game in itself, is divided into five levels. And yes, like you can lose life in a game at any level, death can happen at any level. All one can do is play the game with joy and give your 100%.

Level 0 *ShishuAwastha*: The happy baby phase!

Level 1 *BrahmacharyAshram*: The student life! Full of fun, work, and learning.

Level 2 *GrihasthAshram*: Some people skip this stage altogether. The ones who enter this level, decide to have their own families. The focus is on earning for the family, growing the family, and helping the needy.

Level 3 *VanaprasthAshram*: Retirement time!

Level 4 *SanyaasAshram*: This is a stage where a person is in need of lesser material things, and is happy with whatever little one has. Expectations are very less and so are the needs. The challenges are mainly health-related.

*A game based on this theme is provided at the end of this book **'The Game of Life'**. It is like playing snakes and ladder. Hope you enjoy playing it with your family and friends!*

5. The three human qualities:
We all know that each individual is unique and has peculiar personality traits. They are broadly divided into three buckets[42]:

Satvic: This is where a person is content and happy. There is a level of calmness in this state. There is no one emotion that is extreme.

Rajasik: Where a person feels aggressive, passionate, wants to achieve more, and feels ambitious and proud.

Tamasik: This is where a person feels very lazy, dull and wants to do nothing. This is also a state when one has wrong thoughts flooding the mind.

---

[42] Swami Chinmayananda (2021), Gita for Children, A Teaching Tool for Elders, Chinmaya Prakashan, pg 219.

We all are a cocktail of these traits. And the proportions keep changing over time. Just being aware of our mental state helps us redirect our thoughts and accordingly our actions toward good deeds.

6. About the *Varna* system*:*
Earlier during GES times, society was divided in four categories based on occupations. These were called as *Varnas*. The four categories were:
Brahmin: Educational and religious work
Kshatriya: Security, administration-related work
Vaishya: Trade and business
Shoodra: Service-oriented work

Like in our human body, there are multiple systems working together, can we say the digestive system is superior to the respiratory system? All systems have an important role to play, and the body will stop functioning properly even if one system has a problem. Similarly, the *Varna* system was a healthy ecosystem in itself. There was no clash based on superiority- inferiority of any *Varna*.

The *Varna* system slowly collapsed and is no longer seen in society in its true sense.

7. About the 16 *Sanskaars:*
We all love celebrations, don't we? *Sanatana Dharma* highlights 16 stages/ milestones that typically come in a person's life. These are celebrated or acknowledged in form of rituals. Some of these have lost their relevance over time, but few still play an important role in today's date. *Sanskaars* like the naming ceremony, *Annaprashan, Aksharabhyasa, VBS,* marriage, and the last rituals are some of the prominent 16 Sanskaars still being carried forward.

8. About Rebirth:
Do you know the principle: energy is neither created nor destroyed? On these

lines, it is believed that the energy force within all living beings, is never destroyed. Our body is just an instrument for us to do our *Karma*. The soul is believed to change form, from one body to another[43].

9.	About the law of *Karma:*
	You would have heard 'As you sow, so shall you reap'. Law of Karma tells more or less the same thing. Imagine a mark sheet, where for all good behavior you earn points, and for bad behavior, you get negative points. All your actions are accounted for. Your action is called *Karma*. Positive *Karma* is believed to offer a good life in the next birth[44]. This is one of the beliefs of *Sanatana Dharma.*

10.	What are the objectives in life:

---

[43] Swami Vimalananda (2012), Conflicts and Confusions in Indian Culture, Chinmaya Prakashan, pg 58

[44] Dr. Shyamala Vatsa (2010), A Little Book for The Hindu Child, Fo'c'sle Publications.

It is believed that there are four goals in life[45]:

Dharma: To do what needs to be done. The duties.

Artha: To earn and enjoy wealth but in a rightful way.

Kama: To do things to fulfill own desires, but in rightful ways.

Moksha: This is considered as the ultimate goal in life. To understand and be one with the Ultimate Reality, the Creator[46]! It is believed that *Moksha* frees the soul from the burden of existence.

Look at Hinduism/ Sanatana Dharma as a beautiful lotus flower. The center is where you get to experience the Creator, and all the petals are different beliefs, foundations, and concepts that build and beautify the lotus. We just unfolded a few petals for you. You can of course

---

[45] Roopa Pai (2019), The Vedas and Upanishads for Children, Hachette India, pg 152.

[46] Sadhguru (2020), Death An Inside Story, Penguin Random House India Pvt. Ltd. Pg 109

add more petals based on the child's readiness and your willingness!

The Observation Way:

Today in an urban setting, we often hear parents complaining "My child is using bad words", "My child sings a song but it has the F word", "My child spelled 6 but misplaced the vowel i by e, I was horrified", "My child is always on phone, and just doesn't listen" and so on. Where is the child picking all this from? None other than the environment the child is in!

The digital content around the child is not child friendly, the language people use around the child is full of 'bad words', the songs the child gets to hear are all about love, romance, and breakups, the grown-ups are always with devices. We cannot blame the children. Children are little humans who absorb and learn from their environment right from infancy[47].

During infancy, primary caregivers are the baby's world. Here we cannot stress enough how important early attachment is! Attachment

---

[47] Maria Montessori (2021), The Absorbent Mind, Aakar Books, pg 114.

parenting principles, ensure you are building a strong foundation for the child to turn into a responsible adult[48]. Where the child knows you are the base station to come to in case of problems, even later in life. The child knows he can come to you to seek answers and that he will get genuine replies. The child's early learning happens mainly by observing and imitating the primary caregivers. Hence primary caregivers have a huge responsibility for setting the right examples, values, and boundaries[49].

Yes, the responsibility is huge and can feel overwhelming. Especially when the family size is shrinking, the village needed for the child to grow is shrinking too. Busier parents, unskilled paid help and commercial daycares, make modern-day parenting harder than ever! Hence, having an access to a support community[50], peer

---

[48] William Sears and Martha Sears (2001), The Attachment Parenting Book, Little, Brown & co, USA, pg 19.

[49] Swami Satyananda Saraswati (1999), Yoga Education for Children Volume One, Bihar School of Yoga, pg 68.

[50] Snugbub Mothers Support Community [online]: https://www.snugbub.co.in/mum-support-group

support groups, and forming parent communities in your vicinity proves extremely beneficial. You get the right information, direction, and mental support in this journey of parenting. You are not alone.

As the child grows into a preschooler, he starts having his own opinions, wants, and strong emotions. The child's trusted circle expands. External influences start to matter. Just like in the air we are exposed to various gases along with oxygen. We filter and inhale only the oxygen which we need. Similarly, the child will be **exposed to good, bad, and ugly**. But the right foundation makes it possible for the child to identify good, bad, and ugly, and **filter** out the 'oxygen' he needs! Can you as primary caregivers do anything to help? Well, like how we consciously move away from polluted areas to greener areas to access cleaner air, we can consciously work on exposing the child to a rich environment. Rich in terms of the people and resources he is exposed to. Investing in giving the child varied experiences. More good around, more good absorbed!

The key takeaways for modern-day parenting:

- Having all primary caregivers aligned to core parenting values,
- Responsive, attachment parenting in the early years,
- Access to a robust support community and
- Rich environment for the child to blossom.

In case you align with VBS in principle:

Apart from the above open-ended discussions, you can weave in or go deeper into the various *Sanskaars,* VBS in particular. Help the child understand the 'Why', 'How', 'When', etc. of VBS. This will help the child understand the basis of VBS and form his own opinions around the same. This also ensures that VBS does not become a compulsive act.

Ask for the child's opinion, if the child agrees for VBS. If the child agrees, all preparation done consciously will help the child to not just appreciate VBS, but rather look forward to it.

Also understand, when there is a system, there always will be a few who do not conform to it! And that's fine. In case, the caregivers are ready for VBS but the child is not, please allow the child to discover his own path. Let the caregivers spend more time in this preparatory phase to discuss, debate, and help the child find answers. Ultimately, let the **child's opinion be respected**, whichever way it may be.

***

WHEN CAN VBS BE PERFORMED?

As we discussed in Part One, the question 'When' has different dimensions:

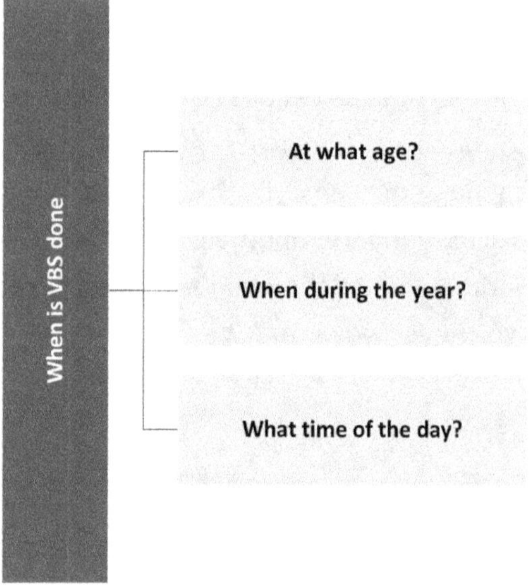

1.   **At what age?**

The best time to perform VBS is when the child is **physically and mentally ready**! Once the child is able to take care of his physical needs with minimal supervision and seems mentally ready to go to the next level- that would be the right time. It will of course vary from child to child. A wide age range in terms of readiness is seen between 5 to 12 years.

Often, when VBS is not done in childhood, is performed right before marriage. It is done from a **marriage eligibility** perspective. After the name-sake VBS ritual, immediately the winding of *BrahmacharyaAshram* is done by performing *Sod Munja (सोड मुंज)'* which is the *Samavartana Sanskaar*. This is nothing less than a mockery of VBS.

2. **When during the year?**

What is the idea behind choosing a particular season for VBS? So that the atmosphere is not extreme and there is happiness in the air. That's how certain seasons were recommended as more suitable than others.

Gauge the environmental conditions of the place you are staying at and pick a time of the year when VBS can be lived and enjoyed by all.

Choose a time period of the year when the child's primary caregivers are under a lesser burden of work/ responsibilities. E.g., Many corporates offer weekly off during the last week of December which would suit the working class, or someone who is a baker might find it more suitable to organize it during Indian festival times when baking orders are very less.

Choose a time of the year that suits your child too. E.g., some kids have issues with heat, and skin irritation during summer. In such a case, it would be right to avoid VBS in summer. If a child is in a mainstream education system, planning VBS during holiday time would be more convenient.

3. **When during the day**

Choose a time when the child is generally happy and active. As long as the child is oriented for VBS and the family is aligned, any time is a good time!

Based on the circadian rhythm of the body, the first half of the day is more suitable, since the energy levels are high and generally everyone is in a happy state of mind.

Beyond this, if one believes in *Muhurta* (auspicious time), it is a good idea to sync it with the above practical aspects as well.

***

CAN WE ALTER THE STEPS OF VBS TO SUIT THE CHANGING TIMES?

When it comes to rituals, we can see three categories of people:

1. Who will accept everything as is, no questions asked;
2. Who will accept a few and object to a few; and
3. Who will question, and implement only when convinced, and modify as needed.

Whichever the category, it is important to remember, VBS is about the **child,** so make sure the child is informed at every step, knows what to expect, and his views are considered in decision-making.

Based on the various steps that form part of VBS, below are some pointers for reflection and planning for each ritual:

Vratas	Points to reflect upon (involving the child)	Possible modification ideas
Nandi and Devpratishtha	Do you believe in doing *Pooja*? Do you have the bandwidth to add this additional step?	If yes, you can include this step. If not, then delegating duties, regular review, and assessment of tasks will help to have better control over the steps leading to VBS and this ritual can be omitted altogether.
Chaul	Is the child comfortable with the idea	If the child is not comfortable, this step can be

	of shaving his head? Does anyone around the child shave their head in a similar way?	omitted. If the family is keen on doing it, a strand of hair can be cut symbolically. Or the child can simply get a regular haircut done before VBS.
Bath	Check if the child is comfortable with others giving him a bath or check if he has a person preference.	Well, these days, taking a daily morning bath itself is becoming irregular in the culture. And hence there is a possibility that the child might contest this step. You can remind the child, how VBS is looked at as a second birth.

		And for that, we need to be physically and mentally clean and fresh. Also, instead of a public bath, the child can take a bath himself. Or based on his consent, a person whom he is comfortable with can give him a bath.
Matrubhojan	This step technically is not relevant anymore, unless the child is leaving for a boarding school/ *Gurukulam*.	As we see more equal parenting and co-parenting, *Matrubhojan* deserves to be turned into *Matru-Pitru Bhojan*! And with diverse

	But one can still include this step, as a symbolic weaning from *ShishuAwastha*	family structures, a *Sneha Bhojan* rather. Instead of an elaborate traditional meal, one can include *satvic* foods from other cuisines which the family enjoys. Even a small spread of favorite dishes which the family relishes together with the right sentiment can do justice to this step.
Mangalashtake	Melody brings joy and that's one of the reasons for	A child who is well-inducted and prepared will be able to appreciate

	including *Mangalashtake*. Many households have their own family *Mangalashtake* which are sung for generations. Discuss within the extended family to find these hidden treasures!	*Mangalashtake* better! Collect some meaningful and melodious *Mangalashtake*. Someone in the family can sing or compose a new one for the child too.
Mekhala-Kaupin	This is mainly a symbolic gesture. Discuss if the child is okay wearing it. Can something more acceptable to the child be	Maybe options like boxer shorts are more comfortable for a child than *Langoti* (underwear). Evaluate similar options as substitutes based on the

	used as a substitute?	child's comfort.
Ajin	A deerskin blanket is definitely not relevant today. Discuss what other options we have today which can also be cruelty-free.	A regular blanket can be gifted to the child instead, based on the weather conditions and preference of the child.
Fire Worship	Fire worship is an important element of VBS. Talk about the symbolic relevance of fire worship	If the child gets an opportunity to observe fire worship at a different place before VBS, it will help to mentally prepare him.
Yagyopavit	*Yagyopavit* is considered important.	You could look at replacing the *Yagyopavit* with

	But are you as caregivers wearing the cotton thread? Does the child have anyone to observe who wears it? If not, is it fair to compel the child to wear it?	a ring or a necklace or earring or something which the child will happily wear[51]. It would do the same job of acting as a reminder and a symbol of the child's 'Second Birth'.
Gayatri Mantra	*Gayatri Mantra* is a powerful *mantra.* But do you chant it regularly? Does the child have anyone to observe who	During the preparation stage, talk to the child about the benefits and importance of *Gayatri Mantra.* If you are not chanting it, maybe chalking

[51] Jynan Prabodhini (2018), Sanskaar Mala Upanayan Sanskaar, Sanskrit Sanskriti Sanshodhika, pg 13

	chants it regularly? Discuss how the child feels and his willingness to chant the *Mantra*.	a family chanting time will help.
Danda	*Danda* is mainly to empower the child towards self-protection. Discuss the importance of self-defense in today's scenario. Discuss various options available that can empower him to protect	Symbolically giving the child a stick as a part of the ritual still opens up possibilities to pick up self-defense in forms like *Silambam*! Discuss with the child what form of martial combat sports he would like to pick up.

	himself.	
Brahmacharya	Refer to the next Section for an elaborate discussion on this topic.	Have an open discussion and shortlist *Vratas* which the child can practically follow. Having a periodical review mechanism and option to revise the *Vratas* is important.
Bhikshaval	This act is no more relevant since the system of *Bhiksha* is outdated. But discuss within the family, how can we incorporate the essence	The *Bhikshaval* can be done symbolically. With a sentiment that in-the-house food will not be wasted, we will co-create a menu that meets our nutrient needs and keeps

	of it in day-to-day life.	choices of all in consideration to some extent.
Poshakh	Discuss what type of clothing is best suited for the place you are in. Considering the lifestyle of the child, discuss what would be the ideal clothing suitable for him.	You can offer suitable and convenient clothing to the child instead of the traditional one. At the same time, no harm in learning how to wear the traditional attire. It actually is very comfortable, minimal, and easy to care for.
Sandhya	Do you as caregivers perform the typical *Sandhya* format	Refer to the next Section for an elaborate discussion on this topic.

	regularly? Does the child have anyone to observe who does it regularly? If not, is it fair to compel the child to do it? Discuss how and what elements of *Sandhya* can be practically incorporated into the child's daily routine.	
Chitrahuti	What rituals do you as a family follow around food? Is there something you can add,	One can look at including some reflection time around meals. Maybe a prayer, observing silence during

	or modify to bring in the essence of expressing gratitude?	meals, or maintaining a gratitude journal, are some ideas that can be easily incorporated[52].
VedArambha – The 12th *Sanskaar* done as a part of VBS today	Discuss if the child would like to know more about the knowledge from our scriptures. If yes there are plenty of resources for children which you can look for. Discuss how languages	If not the scriptures, one can start with simple spoken Sanskrit lessons for the child. A lot of audio-visual content is available for learning Sanskrit along with some institutions that teach Sanskrit to children online as well.

---

[52] *Bharatiya Vichaar Sadhana Pune Prakashan (2022), Hindu Ghar,* pg20.

	evolved. What is unique about the Sanskrit language and how can one benefit from learning it?	

***

ARE THE AGE-OLD VRATAS STILL RELEVANT? CAN WE MODIFY THEM?

Vratas like any other promise is a form of *Tapas* (dedicated action with self-discipline). They hold a significant place in VBS, since these *Vratas* help shape the way of life and imbibe values. But at the same time, sticking to what has been prescribed or practiced for ages may not be relevant in today's times.

Thus, while having a 'Code of Conduct' helps, the Code of Conduct needs to be adapted to the needs of the modern world. One cannot enforce it onto the child. Even if one succeeds to do that, the child may end up brewing a lot of trapped negative emotions. Forget the intended benefits, the child may lose self-confidence and trust.

Hence the best way to have a child agree to certain *Vratas,* is by open discussions which can lead to the **co-creation of Vratas** followed by **willful acceptance**.

Below are some pointers for reflection and planning of *Vratas:*

Vratas	Some points to discuss with your child	More ideas
Self-Cleanliness	How do we keep ourselves clean? Bath/ brushing teeth/ toilet rules etc. What can we do to keep our surroundings clean?	The family together can chalk out the basic cleanliness guidelines. Few tasks could be delegated to the child. E.g.: Kids to maintain an outdoor trip bag. It should have necessary personal hygiene items like sanitizers, tissues, toilet seat covers, travel loo, etc.

Sandhya	Discuss individual beliefs on this topic. Discuss that it is fine if the beliefs do not match and/or change with time. Discuss the purpose of prayer/ meditation. What method of prayer/ meditation does the child want to practice/ try/ explore? What time suits the best for the child for the practice? The time of course	Today, performing morning and evening *Sandhya*, as prescribed traditionally may not be practically feasible for all. Instead, the child can choose an activity that can confer similar benefits. Some examples to consider: guided meditation for kids, *Yoga*, *pranayama*, a prayer of choice with focus and involvement, walking in nature, observing *maun* (silence) at specific times, planning and journaling, etc.

	may vary with circumstances.	
No sleep during the day	Discuss the child's rhythm of the day and find out how much and when the child is sleeping and whether this routine is suiting the needs of the child and family. Discuss the function and role of sleep in our life.	Preschoolers biologically do not **need** a nap and can fulfill their sleep needs at night alone. However, an afternoon nap is a part of many cultures. At times also a family thing. So, evaluate all these aspects and figure out what suits your situation. But note that, if the child naps in the noon, bedtime is bound to get pushed, leading to a late wake-up. You can also

		consult a pediatric sleep coach to chalk out a healthy sleep routine for the child[53].
Being an obedient student	Discuss what teaching-learning means for the family. Where is the child gaining his knowledge from? Who are the child's prominent *Gurus*? What does the child feel about them?	On discussing these points, you will have better clarity on the strengths and weaknesses of the education system that your family has adopted. The same should be openly discussed with the child. The child should be offered an open door to discuss things that are going

[53] Snugbub, Pediatric Sleep Consultations [online] https://www.snugbub.co.in/pediatric-sleep-consultations.

		well or otherwise regarding the chosen system and changes can be made accordingly.
Bhiksha	What are the food-related values you believe in as a family? Discuss food preferences and food diversity. Identify if changes are required in your current food patterns.	The essence of *Bhiksha* was acceptance of food with gratitude. The system is no longer prevalent, but some ideas that can be implemented even today with respect to mindful eating: • Same food for all in the family. 'Family pot' applies to children to grown-ups alike. • Distraction-free

		meals.
		• Wholesome and nutritious food. Plan out days or exceptions when you let loose but let the regular meals be **sans junk aka dead and processed food.**
		• Don't eat for the pleasure of the tongue alone.
		• Don't overeat, listen to your body.
		• Family meals: all family members present at mealtime eat together.
		• These are some examples. You

		can personalize food rules that suit your situation and values.
Sensory Pleasures	Imbibe the message of using sense organs for work and not just for pleasure. Do a time and habit audit to identify gaps.	Review and set boundaries where it is hard for the family, and the child to maintain self-control. E.g., screen time, eating processed food, shopping sprees, etc. Too much of anything is bad!
Other behavioral aspects	Discuss core values you believe in. Discuss what the child feels about them. Introduce the limbs and	Start with smaller goals. Set small challenges for the family. If you are discussing the limbs of *Ashtanga Yoga*, you can, for

	principles of *Ashtanga Yoga* in a child-friendly way. This organically will help different values to seep in. Also, evaluate if the child's emotional needs are met. If the child's needs are unmet, the child can get hooked on what we call 'bad habits over time. Be it the wrong company, negative actions, or addictions.	example, bring in challenges like- Let us practice *Aparigraha* (non-hoarding) this month. Spend some time clearing out wardrobes and segregating must-haves vs. good to have/ not needed. When a family takes up challenges together, it helps the child to stay motivated. In terms of understanding and meeting the child's needs, always keep open communication at regular

		intervals to check on each other. Regularly spend quality time with the child.
Agni Pooja	Discuss about the *Panchamahabhutas* (Five elements of nature) Discuss the role of the fire element. Discuss the ingredients used for *Agni Pooja*. If the family believes in *Ahimsa* discuss what could be the possible alternatives for dairy	Agni Pooja is not relevant in the majority of cases today. Hence this *vrata* can be completely omitted from the daily to-do list unless one is on the path that calls for this practice. However, fire element in certain forms can definitely be incorporated into a few daily rituals. For e.g.: • Lighting a lamp during

	ingredients/ cutting firewood.	*Yoga* practice. • Guiding the child to do *Trataka Pranayama* with the help of a candle/ lamp. • Giving the responsibility of switching on lights in the house every evening when it gets dark. • Lighting a lamp during whichever form of *Sandhya* practice the child has chosen to do.

Apart from the *Vratas* traditionally prescribed for children, below are a few *Vratas* which a family can sign up for based on today's needs and circumstances:

Vratas	Some points to discuss with your child	More ideas
Generate minimal solid waste	• How is waste a big concern today? • What is a landfill? • Audit your daily waste and find out what could have been avoided. • What can be done to generate lesser daily waste in the house?	Few ideas one can implement and allocate some responsibilities to the child: • Follow the Refuse – Reuse – Recycle – Repair formula. • Carry your own containers/ bags for shopping. • Compost wet waste. • Use reusable cutlery instead of disposable ones.

		• Carry your own reusable water bottles. • Buy groceries in bigger portions than smaller packets wherever possible.
Toward the Earth's green cover	With the kind of space available and interest, discuss with the child, how can he contribute to maintaining/ increasing the green cover in and around your house.	Some ideas to consider: • Grow microgreens. • Grow other edibles. • Participate in tree plantation activities. • Get involved in community gardening initiatives. • Adopt a tree and care for it.
Mindful consumeris	• Discuss with the child about your	A child can take this Vrata in different ways

m	strengths and weaknesses when it comes to purchasing things. • Discuss money. • Discuss how the total income is broadly distributed in various output streams in your household (groceries, commute, donations, food, shopping, etc.) • Pick a month and review the purchases that were avoidable, and talk about it openly with	depending on their age and understanding. Some ideas: • Managing finance for a trip. • Regular expense audit and identifying purchases that were avoidable. • Getting involved in a thrift store or starting one in your community. • Maintaining cashflow for oneself.

	your child. • Watch documentaries on money/ minimalism/ consumerism with your child.	
Digital Detox	Discuss how much time is spent on devices and how much of it is spent *on* **media as a resource**. Audit your screen time and find out areas of improvement.	Based on the outcomes of the screentime audit, the family can decide on some boundaries as may be necessary. Discuss with the child various aspects of cyber security too.
Social Service	Discuss with your child about socio-economic differences. Talk about different ways in which	Few ideas the family can look at: • Starting from home, being kind and

	one can contribute to the betterment of society.	compassionate towards other family members and house help. • Participating/ conducting toys/ clothes donation camps. • Volunteering at various philanthropic activities.
Household chores	List out common chores. List out individual responsibilities and the flow of the day. Discuss how running a house is teamwork and work distribution is important so that no one	Running a house is like keeping a system alive in a healthy way, where each person holds a place and has a role. Encourage the child to take up small chores like: • Washing own dishes, • Putting dirty laundry for

	person is overburdened.	washing, • Drying clothes, • Folding/ keeping back clothes in the cupboard, • Taking care of pets, • Helping in the kitchen, • Gardening, • Washing vehicles, etc.
Water conservation	• Discuss water as a resource, and how it is getting negatively impacted today. • Use different resources like books, documentaries, and people who can help sensitize children about	Based on the discussions, figure out ways where you can reduce water usage/ reuse grey water, and employ rainwater harvesting. Let the child be involved actively in planning and execution.

	this topic. • Audit your family's water usage.	

And remember, the easiest way to see any change in children is to 'Practice what we preach'!

***

SUMMARY

VBS is a great tool to shape the next generation. But VBS is not a magic wand. Just by performing VBS, one cannot expect the child to suddenly become independent, sharp, and intelligent. VBS paves the way, sets the ground, and curates the child to be ready for the next level. In today's times, primary caregivers' responsibility does not end by simply performing VBS. It is a commitment to walk the path with the child if the child is growing up with them. A house cannot have two divisions, one where the child is expected to follow a certain level of discipline and the other where the primary caregivers are having a life without boundaries! Either party will end up syncing with the other. In the interest of all, it is better if the primary caregivers are in sync with the child's path than the opposite.

The recipe for VBS that can be transformative?

The right preparation, signing up for suitable *Vratas*, family working as a team, having the right *Purohit*, formulating and following a value system to cater to the changing needs of the family in the coming years.

The below flowchart summarizes the crux of action points for caregivers as a roadmap!

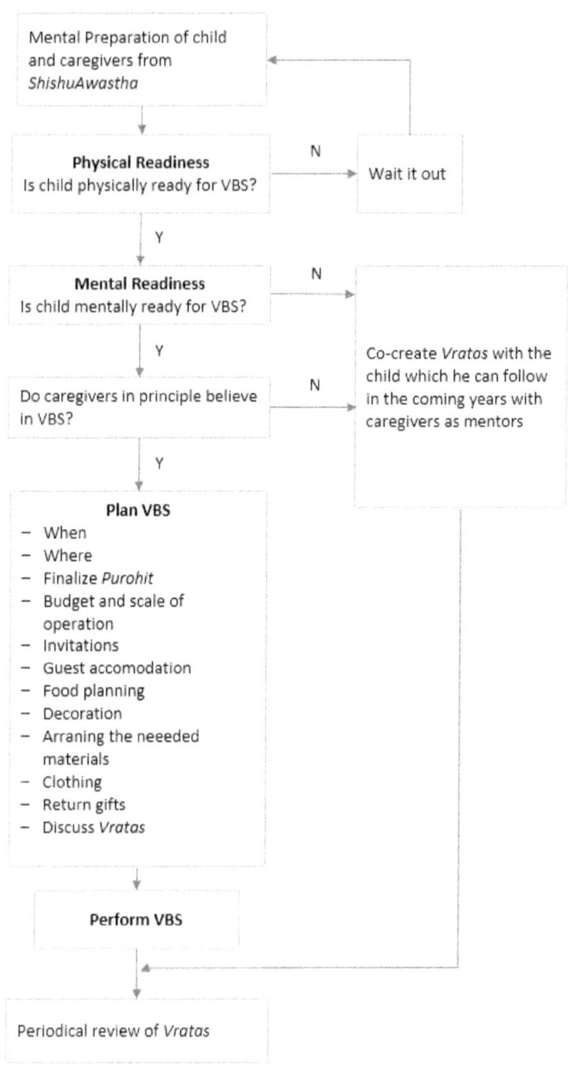

Mental Preparation of child and caregivers from ShishuAwastha
Physical Readiness
Is child physically ready for VBS?
N
Wait it out
Y
Mental Readiness
Is child mentally ready for VBS?
N
Y
Do caregivers in principle believe in VBS?
N
Co-create Vratas with the child which he can follow in the coming years with caregivers as mentors
Y
Plan VBS
— When
— Where
— Finalize Purohit
— Budget and scale of operation
— Invitations
— Guest accomodation
— Food planning
— Decoration
— Arraning the neeeded materials
— Clothing
— Return gifts
— Discuss Vratas
Perform VBS
Periodical review of Vratas

* * *

THE GAME OF LIFE

Snakes and Ladders –

Scan the QR code for the downloadable version of the game!

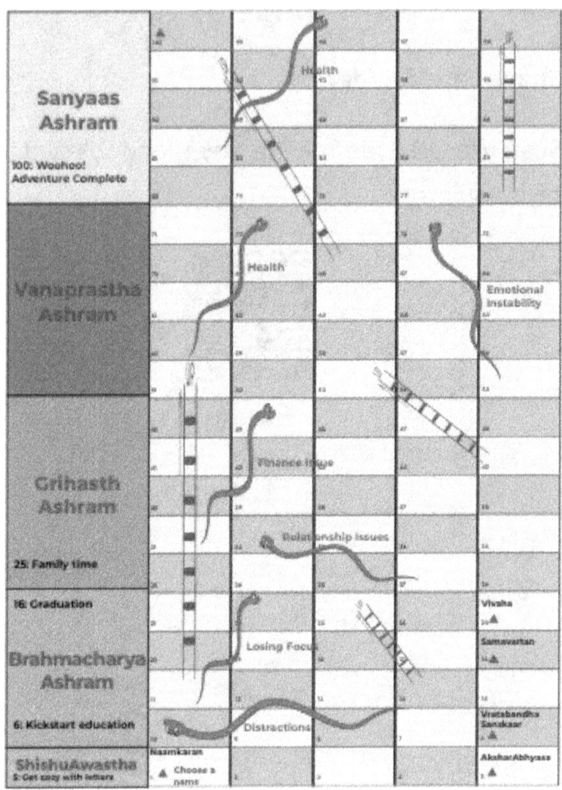
Sanyaas Ashram
100: Woohoo! Adventure Complete
Health
Vanaprastha Ashram
Health
Emotional Instability
Grihasth Ashram
Finance Issue
25: Family time
Relationship Issues
16: Graduation
Viwaha
Losing Focus
Samavartan
Brahmacharya Ashram
6: Kickstart education
Vratabandha Sanskaar
Distractions
Naamkaran
Choose a name
ShishuAvastha
5: Get easy with letters
Akshar Abhyaas

***

ACKNOWLEDGMENTS

I cannot explain how and why I became the instrument to bring the information on *Vratabandha Sanskaar* to you all. I express my gratitude to the higher power for enabling me to accomplish this task.

I thank my family, for allowing me the time and space to take this journey. This being an alien subject to me a couple of years back, it did need a lot of research, talking to people, visiting places, taking notes, listening to talks, and so on. My family wholeheartedly supported me and also participated in the process in their own ways!

I thank my friends, the *Gurus,* and critics for all their support and contribution towards this book.

May this book be the medium for constructive changes in children, families, and society at large.

176

***

REFERENCES

Arranged Alphabetically

1. A.C. Bhaktivedanta Swami Prabhupada (2018), Basics of Bhagwad-Gita, The Bhaktivedanta Book Trust.

2. A.C. Bhaktivedanta Swami Prabhupada (1972), Bhagavad Gita as it is, The Bhaktivedanta Book Trust.

3. Aditya Singh, Subjects Taught in Gurukul Education System [online], https://vediconcepts.com/subjects-taught-in-a-gurukul/. (last accessed on 25 November 2022)

4. Bharatiya Vichaar Sadhana Pune Prakashan (2022), Hindu Ghar.

5. Central Chinmaya Mission Trust (2019), Hinduism: Frequently Asked Questions, Chinmaya Prakashan.

6. ChinamayaChannel, Bhagavad Geeta - Death & Rebirth (Chapter 2 Verse 22) https://www.youtube.com/watch?v=Dy-QLmh_yjY. (last accessed on 25 November 2022)

7. ChinamayaChannel, Should The Teacher Carry You To Heaven? - Lift Yourself! - Chapter 6 Verse 5 [online] https://youtu.be/b8iynPEW3oU. (last accessed on 25 November 2022)

8. Dr. Shyamala Vatsa (2010), A Little Book for The Hindu Child, Fo'c'sle Publications.

9. Federal Center for Health Education, Sexuality Education Policy Brief No. 1 [online] https://www.euro.who.int/__data/assets/pdf_file/0008/379043/Sexuality_education_Policy_brief_No_1.pdf. (last accessed on 25 November 2022)

10. Immortal Bharat [online], https://www.immortalbharat.in/2020/07/how-british-destroyed-indian-education.html. (last accessed on 25 November 2022)

11. Immortal Bharat, Part 1 - Education in Ancient India [online], https://youtu.be/M79C3dSB90A. (last accessed on 25 November 2022)

12. K. A. Manoj Narayanan, N. Venugopalan (2018). Effect of Gayatri mantra chanting on cognitive functions in school children. Int J Pediatr Res;5(3):113-115. doi:10.17511/ijpr.2018.3.03.

13. Jynan Prabodhini (2018), Sanskaar Mala Upanayan Sanskaar, Sanskrit Sanskriti Sanshodhika.

14. Maria Montessori (2021), The Absorbent Mind, Aakar Books.

15. Michel Danimo (Third Edition 2011), The Invasion That Never Was, Vivekananda Kendra Prakashan Trust.

16. Palki Sharma, Macaulay Education System, Colonialisation & Inferiority complex in India Explained [online], https://youtu.be/SEseHkMwPSM. (last accessed on 25 November 2022)

17. Pradhan B, Derle SG (2012). Comparison of the effect of Gayatri Mantra and Poem Chanting on

Digit Letter Substitution Task. Anc Sci Life; 32(2):89-92. doi:10.4103/0257-7941.118540. PMID: 24167333; PMCID: PMC3807963.

18. Pradnya Jere & Y. S. Lele (2003), Dharmavidhinchya Antarangat, Sanskrit Sanskriti Sanshodhika

19. Rajbali Pandey (2018), Hindu Samskaras; Socio-Religious Study of the Hindu Sacraments, Motilal Banarasidas Publishers Pvt. Ltd.

20. Rajeev, Gayatri Mantra – Meaning, Significance and Benefits [online], https://vedicfeed.com/gayatri-mantra-meaning-significance-and-benefits/. (last accessed on 25 November 2022)

21. Rajiv Dixit, Macaulay Destroyed Ancient Indian (Guru-Shishya) Education System [online], https://www.youtube.com/watch?v=q9N68QDyEbl&t=1143s. (last accessed on 25 November 2022)

22. Rashtra Sevika Samiti (2011), Upanayan Sansaar, Shodh va Bodh.

23. Ravindra Bodhe (2021), Yoga and Value Education, O. P. Tiwari Kaivalyadham.

24. Roopa Pai (2019), The Vedas and Upanishads for Children, Hachette India.

25. Sadhguru (2020), Death An Inside Story, Penguin Random House India Pvt. Ltd.

26. Sadhguru (2021), Life and Death in One Breath, Jaico Publishing House.

27. Sahana Singh (2017), The Educational Heritage of Ancient India How An Ecosystem of Learning Was Laid to Waste, Notion Press.

28. Sahana Singh (2022), Revisiting the Educational Heritage of India, Vitasta Publishing Pvt. Ltd.

29. Sanatan Says, Are We Hindus? by Swami Sampatidasa [online] https://www.youtube.com/shorts/GxfKNfbZHpM. (last accessed on 25 November 2022)

30. Sarala Nirmal (2021), Salutations to You! Oh Death!, Mythree Samprathishtaana.

31. Sinu Joseph (2017), Should Women Chant The Gayatri Mantra? [online] https://mythrispeaks.wordpress.com/2017/03/08/should-women-chant-the-gayatri-mantra/. (last accessed on 25 November 2022)

32. Snugbub Mothers Support Community [online]: https://www.snugbub.co.in/mum-support-group. (last accessed on 25 November 2022)

33. Snugbub, Pediatric Sleep Consultations [online] https://www.snugbub.co.in/pediatric-sleep-consultations. (last accessed on 25 November 2022)

34. Sri Ramanasramam- Upanayanam [online], https://ramana-talk-mailer.appspot.com/read?post_name=Letter&index=124. (last accessed on 25 November 2022)

35. Swami Chinmayananda (2021), Gita for Children, A Teaching Tool for Elders, Chinmaya Prakashan.

36. Swami Satyananda Saraswati (1999), Yoga Education for Children Volume One, Bihar School of Yoga.

37. Swami Tejomayananda (2022), Dharma Shastra, Way to Peace, Prosperity and Purity, Chinmaya Prakashan.

38. Swami Vimalananda (2012), Conflicts and Confusions in Indian Culture, Chinmaya Prakashan.

39. Swami Vimalananda (2019), Hinduism: Frequently Asked Questions, Central Chinmaya Prakashan.

40. Swami Vimalananda & Radhika Krishnakumar (2019), In Indian Culture, Why Do We, Chinmaya Prakashan.

41. Swami Vivekananda (2022), The Complete Book of Yoga, FingerPrint Life.

42. Swati Chanchani & Rajiv Chanchani (2021), Yoga for Children, CBS Publishers & Distributors.

43. V. L. Manjul, Starting Vedic Studies [online], https://www.hinduismtoday.com/magazine/october-november-december-2002/2002-10-starting-vedic-studies/. (last accessed on 25 November 2022)

44. Vedanta Kesari, Education: A Ramakrishna-Vivekananda Perspective [online] https://www.swamivivekananda.guru/2021/05/12/education-a-ramakrishna-vivekananda-perspective/. (last accessed on 25 November 2022)

45. Wikipedia The Free Encyclopedia, Sadhguru, [online] https://en.wikipedia.org/wiki/Sadhguru. (last accessed on 25 November 2022)

46.   William Sears and Martha Sears (2001), The Attachment Parenting Book, Little, Brown & co, USA.

***

www.ingramcontent.com/pod-product-compliance
Lightning Source LLC
Chambersburg PA
CBHW070517160726
48003CB00004B/1601